1·75

C000174664

Traditional Herb & Spice Cookery

# TRADITIONAL
# HERB & SPICE
## COOKERY

*Jack Santa Maria*

Illustrations by John Spencer

## RIDER

London Melbourne Sydney Auckland Johannesburg

Rider and Company
An imprint of Century Hutchinson Ltd

17–21 Conway Street, London W1P 6JD

Hutchinson Publishing Group (Australia) Pty Ltd
PO Box 496, Hawthorn, Melbourne, Victoria 3122

Hutchinson Group (NZ) Ltd
PO Box 40–086, Glenfield 10, Auckland

Hutchinson Group (SA) Pty Ltd
PO Box 337, Bergvlei, 2012 South Africa

First published 1985
© Jack Santa Maria 1985
Illustrations © John Spencer 1985

Set in Linotron Goudy
by Wyvern Typesetting Limited, Bristol

Printed and bound in Great Britain
by Guernsey Press Co. Ltd.
Guernsey, C.I.

British Library Cataloguing in Publication Data

Santa Maria, Jack
Traditional herb and spice cookery.
1. Cookery (Spices)   2. Cookery (Herbs)
I. Title
641.6'383     TX819.A1

ISBN 0 7126 1075 8

# Contents

# ACKNOWLEDGEMENTS

The author would like to thank the following: Mr P. S. Morrish, sub-librarian at the Brotherton Library, Leeds University, for his help in selecting books from the John F. Preston Collection; Margaret Rooney, for testing many of the recipes; Kate Simunek, for the loan of *Mrs Cole's Cookery*; and Jo Edwards and Esther Jagger for their invaluable help in preparing the typescript for publication.

# Introduction: The Grand Puzzle

But in spite of our receipts and our philosophy, the briskness of the fire, the skill of our cook, the excellence of the oven, and the bright array of pots, kettles, pans, moulds, griddles and gridirons . . . or the most rigid scale and measure of economy, one grand puzzle besets alike all kitchens – the difficulty of really getting the ingredients on which the mystery of food manufacture is to be exercised.

Frederick Briggs, *The Illustrated London Cookery Book*, 1852

Since Stone Age times, England has been in a position to supply her inhabitants with a well-balanced, wholefood diet of cereals, dairy produce, meat, fish, pulses, vegetables and fruit, with honey (originally) the principal sweetener, and salt and aromatic herbs the preservatives and flavourings. The Romans augmented it with a range of new herbs and spices which they brought with them, and since then hundreds of these plants have played a role both in preserving food and in enhancing it to create variety and to appeal to different tastes.

There is nothing new about food additives, then, but it is their nature that has radically changed over the centuries.

As England moved out of the depression of the Dark Ages that followed the departure of the Romans, the cultural mood of the medieval period – the time when the great cathedrals were being built – was one of optimism. Eating habits reflected this mood, and England became known as a place for good eating, particularly among the wealthy. Meat, fish, poultry and game were cooked with great diversity and ingenuity, and with generous use of herbs, spices and fruit. When Andrew Boorde wrote: 'There is no herb, nor weed, but God hath given virtue to them, to help man' (*A Dyetary of Helth*, 1542), he summed up the attitude towards plants that prevailed in the Middle Ages and was still current in the sixteenth century. The cottager put to some culinary or medicinal purpose most of the plants which grew in his garden or round about in the fields and woods, and at that time over one hundred herbs were in common use.

Even at this early stage, however, undesirable additives were finding their way into English food. The addition of useless ingredients to food products in order to gain weight and thereby increase profits is probably as old as trade itself. In the fourteenth century, when the spice trade became centred in London, it was organized by the Guild of Pepperers, later called the Grocers (from *grossarii*, the dealers in bulk or *en gros* transactions). In

1316 the Pepperers had drawn up a set of rules to discourage the adulteration of food products. Later, the Grocers undertook to sift the bales of spices from abroad to uncover any rubbish (known as garble) added to increase weight and bulk.

For several centuries England depended on foreign merchants for the supply of spices. Such was their value that it was often possible to pay one's rent in spices, which gave rise to the term 'peppercorn rent'. (Today it would take a lot of pepper to pay your rent or mortgage!) During the seventeenth century, when saffron was still one of the favourite flavouring and colouring spices, the careful housewife kept her costly spices locked in small, separate drawers in wooden spice cupboards. Then, during the eighteenth century, as England gained larger footholds in the West Indies and the Far East, foreign domination of the world trade in cloves, nutmeg, pepper and cinnamon collapsed.

Sophisticated cookery in Tudor times tended to be confined to the manor houses and fortified homes of the nobility. England's first printed cookery book, *The Boke of Cokery*, appeared in 1500 and was intended for these wealthy households. Previously, before the invention of printing, cookery books had been produced in handwritten manuscript form. Soon more books started to appear, addressed to the woman of the house, with such titles as *The Good Huswifes Jewell*, *The Good Hous-Wives Treasurie* and *The Good Huswives Handmaid*. These sixteenth-century books were still written by men, as they continued to be for another hundred years. It was not considered auspicious for the country housewife to share her culinary secrets with the outside world. Such was the mystery surrounding kitchen lore that it was felt that these skills might be literally lost if they were given away.

In the seventeenth century, the traditional cookery of England was still the envy of her European neighbours and a constant source of discussion among the cooks and cookery writers of France and Italy. Then two things happened to change this state of affairs. During the eighteenth century England, like other European countries, experienced a vogue for everything French, including her cookery. And towards the end of that century, with increasing industrialization of what had formerly been cottage industries, bottled sauces and pickles began to be produced on a commercial scale. So in wealthy houses England's natural gastronomic traditions were deserted in favour of the new French cuisine, and at the other end of the social scale there was no longer any necessity for the housewife to prepare dishes with the traditional herbs and spices, since these flavours could much more simply be added to one's food on the plate.

There were two further contributory factors to this decline in the standard of English food. By the end of the eighteenth century England had a virtual monopoly in the West Indian sugar trade. As a result sugar became very cheap and ousted honey as the main sweetener. Sugar made bland foods more appetizing and it sweetened bitter ones, so that people had less need of the stimulus of spices. It was also addictive, and inhibited people's ability to digest the fibre in wholemeal bread. As a result, the demand for white bread arose. 'Refined' food had arrived. The English started to use sugar virtually as a 'spice' in all branches of cookery – it was sprinkled on meat, fish, pies and tarts, as well as being included in the dish itself. But, ironically, the very popularity of sugar made it a target for the food adulterators. Only a hundred years ago, cookery writers were complaining that it was being mixed with chalk, sand, clay and flour.

The second factor was that from the mid-eighteenth century, as the Industrial Revolution developed, there was an increasing migration from the countryside to the towns. Rural traditions of cookery were neglected, because factory labour, in which the whole family was often involved, left little time for the preparation of food. Workers were often paid in tokens which could only be spent at the factory shop, which stocked only poor-quality, unhealthy, additive-ridden food.

As with all fashions, it did not take long before a reaction to the new popularity of French cookery developed in a few of the more privileged homes of Britain. This was also the time when women were emerging from their self-imposed silence on such matters and starting to produce some of the classic cookery books of the day. In 1747 Hannah Glasse remarked, 'If gentlemen will have French cooks, they must pay for French tricks.' In *The Art of Cookery* she campaigned for more encouragement for English cooks and less pandering to French fashion. Eliza Smith also realized the dangers of abandoning English tradition and wrote, 'To our disgrace, we admired the French tongue and the French messes' (*The Compleat Housewife*, 1750). Samuel Johnson, however, voiced some of his contemporaries' fears of these outspoken female writers when he said that 'Women can spin very well, but they cannot write a good book of cookery.' Yet from the early eighteenth century until the present day, women have been writing some of the best-selling cookery books.

In the nineteenth century English publishers brought out book after book on the domestic arts. Longmans thwarted Eliza Acton's dreams of becoming a poet and persuaded her to write *Modern Cookery*, published in 1845. Sixteen years later, Isabella Beeton's celebrated *Book of Household Management* appeared when she was only twenty-four. The first edition weighed around 3 lb (1.4 kg) and, along with the family Bible, found pride of place in many Victorian households. Sadly, its author died only four years later.

During the nineteenth century English cookery was still in decline however. The industrial masses were no longer practising the old traditions, and French culture remained predominant among the rich. French became the language of diplomacy, the kitchen and the restaurant, and in spite of the efforts of many writers to preserve traditional dishes, their unpopularity continued.

The Great Exhibition at the Crystal Palace in 1851 showed that Britain was lagging behind the other industrial nations in developing and using new technology. For centuries the structure of society had been thought of as part of some divine plan (as expressed in the words of the hymn 'All Things Bright and Beautiful'), which illiteracy among the poorer classes had helped to maintain. But now the ability to read was seen as the key to progress, and the Education Acts of 1870 and 1902 were designed to bring about universal literacy. Now recipe books could be used more widely. In addition, different generations of the same family were beginning to live apart from each other, so that the mother was no longer necessarily there to teach her daughters how to cook; as a result the market for cookery books increased further.

These cookery books have proved to be valuable historical and sociological documents. They show, for example, that by the late nineteenth century, while food was being consumed in vast quantities in wealthy households, many people in the new towns as well as the countryside were suffering a poor, imbalanced diet.

The two World Wars seemed to have left England in the culinary doldrums. People had grown used to dried egg, margarine, food rationing and in general a greasy, watery repertoire with flavour and quality either left out or cooked out. After 1945, many writers suggested that good cookery could only be revived if cooks would imitate the good, earthy dishes of the French or Italian peasants. Since the peasantry of England and many of its traditions had been wiped out in a hundred years of industrial development, there was some sense in these suggestions. Other writers tried to show that in rural areas much traditional English cookery from before the nineteenth century had in fact survived. Not only that, but many new dishes had been created since then by the people of the industrial towns and cities, who needed to provide economical yet tasty food for their families.

What is thought of now as traditional English fare includes a number of dishes which are rich in sugar and fats. But they came into the repertoire in response to the needs of poorly paid manual workers, working long hours in cold surroundings, and often living in cold, damp homes. Many of those conditions have now changed. Far fewer people are engaged in heavy manual labour, which burns off large amounts of calories; many of us do sedentary jobs and take little exercise. In addition, most of us now live in warm homes and we do not burn calories just in the effort of keeping warm. Because of our change of lifestyle, many of these more solid traditional dishes should be eaten only in moderation or in conjunction with a proper programme of exercise. Indeed some nutritionists now consider that our ideal diet would be mainly vegetarian, with meat and fish appearing mainly in soups or sauces, or no more than once or twice a week as a main course. Such a diet would make meat-eating more of an occasion, calling for recipes with something special to offer.

Today the problem for the cook is not so much a lack of guidance in the English tradition, or a lack of ingredients, but rather that the ingredients are full of other, less desirable components. Although most food is considered pure and fit for human consumption, it contains a whole new range of products that are termed 'useful' because they are designed to benefit the consumer. Many of these products have taken over the traditional roles played by herbs and spices: they may preserve the shelf life of a food, make it look more appetizing, or give it the colour and flavour taken out during processing.

The consumer is assured that cheap food produced on a large scale means that animals must be bred and reared as if they were food-producing machines. These animals are injected with growth hormones, vaccines and, later, chemicals to make their flesh gain weight through absorbing water, itself an additive. The meat is treated with preservatives, tenderizers and colorants. Even plants are grown in factory-like conditions. Vegetables and fruit are sprayed with pesticides, fungicides and weedkillers while growing, and later treated with hormones, preservatives, colorants and waxes. Many of these products are, inevitably, consumed along with the food. This new adulteration of food may be necessary in our fast-moving and demanding commercial world, but the value of many food additives is being seriously questioned on health, economic and even moral grounds.

In 1861, unaware of such developments, but conscious of the demise of traditional English cookery, Isabella Beeton wrote, 'One great cause of many spoilt dishes and badly cooked meats arises, we think, from a non-acquaintance with common, everyday things.' In spite of the overwhelming pressure to eat nothing but commercially produced convenience foods, many people today are looking for those 'common, everyday things', i.e. the feel and smell of fresh ingredients. The caring cook will be wary of the use of additives by food-producers, will use wholefoods whenever possible, and will take time and trouble to prepare good, wholesome fare.

This book shows how, by using traditional herb and spice recipes that have been adapted to modern needs, vital ingredients may be put back into English cookery. It will introduce you to 'new' ways of roasting meat and of cooking fish and vegetables; of mixing tasty stuffings and sauces; of baking traditional pies and concocting drinks. It describes how food has always played a special part in the English calendar. Most of all, it encourages you to look for those 'common, everyday things' that bring the real joy of cookery. And joy is an ingredient too.

Most of the recipes in books on traditional English cookery published in the 1950s can be traced back to those published in the late eighteenth century. These in turn can be traced to authors who were writing at least fifty years before, such as Hannah Glasse. So there is a link between the traditional recipes in current use and those which were written down before the Industrial Revolution got under way. Traditional English cookery boasts a great range of tasty dishes, from those that fill, warm and nourish to those that are light and full of zest. The recipes here are taken from this great tradition and concentrate specifically on herb and spice cookery. This collection is a tribute to the cooks and cookery writers of the past who have brought imagination, flavour, aroma and wholesomeness to the English table.

# A Directory of Herbs & Spices

The first record in England of an imported spice or flavouring herb of Mediterranean origin occurs in the late Bronze Age (c. 500 BC), when coriander was brought by immigrants to flavour barley gruel. Much later, several herbs were introduced as garden plants to supply the needs of the Roman settlers; they included alexanders, borage, chervil, coriander, dill, fennel, garlic, hyssop, leek, mint, onion, parsley, rosemary, rue, sage, savory, sweet marjoram and thyme.

The Romans also brought with them cassia, cinnamon, ginger and pepper, of which pepper was the most popular. The supply of pepper and other spices was interrupted in the fifth century and did not pick up again until the eighth century when supplies began to arrive via Germany. Pepper then became so common that the pepper-horn was considered a necessary utensil in the English farmhouse.

With the advent of Norman cookery in England, the use of spices increased. Nutmeg, mace and cloves were some of the new spices that had hardly been known in Roman times. Along with pepper, these became the basis of the European spice trade. Herbs continued to be cultivated in medieval England. They were also gathered wild for culinary and medicinal uses. Parsley was now the most popular flavouring herb and coriander, enjoyed by the Romans, came to be used more and more as a medicinal herb and less as a potherb.

By the end of the seventeenth century, the aromatic herbs of Mediterranean origin had gained prominence over the indigenous English ones. The faggot of sweet herbs, or *bouquet garni* of the French, became the standard herbal addition to most dishes. The position remained the same for another two hundred years when interest in other herbs was revived.

During this century, as supplies became more costly and irregular, spices were used to prepare pickles which were then used to season dishes instead of the spices themselves. The amount of spice put into cakes and puddings also began to diminish. Towards the end of the eighteenth century, bottled sauces and pickles were being produced on a commercial scale.

Today, herbs and spices are no longer required to mask the unpleasant flavours of stale, oversalted or badly preserved food. However, they can be used to advantage in small quantities to enhance flavour in a subtle way in both savoury and sweet dishes.

It is now possible to buy a very large range of herbs in wholefood and herbal stores, but there is nothing like a fresh herb! Indeed some herbs, like parsley, lose nearly all their flavour when dried, so are particulary worth growing. The majority of them require very little effort to cultivate, though they do need good drainage and a warm soil temperature. Prepare the soil in the autumn and start planting in the spring. Mint needs to be kept within bounds in its own tub since its growth is so vigorous. If you do not have a garden, use pots and window boxes. Many herbs do well in such situations, provided they get plenty of sunlight.

Buy spices in small quantities and store them in airtight containers away from the light. Dried herbs should also be stored in this way since they too will quickly lose their aromatic properties.

Below, arranged alphabetically, are a few notes on the herbs and spices used in this book. Be prepared to try new ones as you come across them and do not feel restricted to the ones mentioned here. For four people 1–3 tablespoons of chopped fresh herbs are usually sufficient in a recipe. About 1 teaspoon of dried crushed herbs is equivalent to a tablespoon of chopped fresh herbs.

ALLSPICE. *Pimenta dioica* resembles large brown peppercorns – the unripe berries are picked and then dried in the sun. Its warm, peppery taste is said to be like a combination of nutmeg, clove and cinnamon. It has been popular in England since the seventeenth century. It is best to buy the whole spice and store it in an airtight jar where it will keep almost indefinitely. Allspice is a digestive and carminative with mild anti-bacterial properties. It should not be confused with 'mixed spice'.

Use allspice in both savoury and sweet dishes, including cakes.

BASIL. *Ocicum basilicum* is a strongly flavoured, sweetly aromatic herb. It will grow in England in a sunny, sheltered position. Fresh basil is good in salads, with tomatoes, eggs and mushrooms, and with certain fish such as sole.

Use in basting sauces, biscuits, breads, herb butter, cheese, and fruit and wine cups; and with eggs, fish, game, lamb and mutton, pork and ham, poultry, and as a garnish.

BAY. The smooth, leathery leaves of the bay tree, *Laurus nobilis*, are dark green on top and lighter underneath. Bay has a warm, resinous bouquet with a slightly bitter flavour, so use it sparingly. Buy whole dried leaves, not powdered ones, and make sure they are green – brown ones will have lost their flavour. An evergreen shrub or tree of the Mediterranean, the bay tree can grow in warm areas of England to provide a year-round supply of fresh bay leaves. It is one of the ingredients in a 'bunch of sweet herbs' and seems to have been cultivated in England since the sixteenth century. Do not confuse bay with the common laurel, *Prunus lauracerasus*, which is highly poisonous. This plant has the characteristic almond-like bouquet of cyanide.

Use in basting sauces when roasting a joint, in custards and milk puddings, jellies and creams; and with game, beef, lamb and mutton, offal, poultry, and as a garnish.

BORAGE. *Borago officinalis* is a tall, hairy-leaved plant with blue, star-shaped flowers. Used in traditional medicine as a tonic, the young leaves may be chopped to put in salads. The leaves and flowers are excellent in a wine or cider cup, imparting a flavour somewhat like cucumber. The leaves can also be used to make a refreshing hot tea.

BUNCH OF SWEET HERBS

Are you going to Scarborough Fair?
Parsley, sage, rosemary and thyme.

The words of the traditional song *Scarborough Fair* contain the ingredients, which of course may be varied according to taste. The 'bunch of sweet herbs', also occurring in old cookery books as a 'bundle of sweet herbs' or a 'faggot of herbs', should be tied together so that it can be removed at the end of the cooking. If you wish to add spices or pieces of citrus peel or garlic to your 'bunch', the various ingredients are better enclosed in a little muslin bag. Many cooks include a bay leaf along with the stalks of parsley and a sprig of sage or thyme. Your own choice of herbs will give an individual flavour to your cookery.

CAPERS. A trailing shrub, native to the Mediterranean and Middle East, *Capparis spinosa* can be grown in England in a greenhouse. The unopened flower buds have been used as a condiment for thousands of years. They are salted and pickled in vinegar. Good capers should be dark green with a small piece of stalk attached.

Capers may be used in fish dishes, with lamb and game, and in caper sauces.

CARAWAY. The light or dark brown seeds of *Carum carvi* are available whole. They have a sweet, warm, aromatic bouquet which is slightly peppery. Caraway seeds were used in Elizabethan times to flavour breads, cakes and fruit, especially apples. They reached their height of popularity in the eighteenth and early nineteenth centuries.

Caraway water, like dill water, is well known for its carminative effect, especially for babies. 'Caraway', the Elizabethan gardener Langham observed in 1579, 'breaketh winde'.

The plant can be grown in England like dill and fennel, as long as it has a sunny aspect. The leaves can be chopped and added to salads or used as a garnish. They were often used by the cottage gardener and smallholder to keep chickens from straying, since they are attracted to caraway. Use the seeds in biscuits, bread and cakes, and with cheese, pork and ham.

CAYENNE, CHILLI. Cayenne pepper is a finely ground powder prepared from the seeds and pods of various types of chilli, *Capsicum frutescens*. As most powders are blends, the names of the varieties are not very important. Cayenne, a red or red-brown powder, is hot and pungent, though not as powerful as the hotter chillies. It is mainly distinguished from chilli powder by being more finely ground. Cayenne takes its name from its supposed place of origin, the Cayenne region of the colony of French Guiana, though it is now largely grown in Africa, Mexico and the USA. Chillies have been cultivated in South America since prehistoric times.

An ingredient of Worcestershire sauce, chilli is healthful in small amounts, because it is a digestive and an intestinal and gastric tonic. These properties have been confirmed by research in India, revealed in 1984. Chilli powder is easily made at home by grinding dried red chillies to the required texture.

Chilli adds piquancy to stews, casseroles, sauces, seafood dishes and roast meats. Sprinkle it on bacon before frying, and add it when seasoning flour to coat food that is to be fried.

CELERY. The green or brown seeds of *Apium graveolens dulce* have a warm, bitter flavour. They are a spice of the western world which can be used in any dish which needs the taste of celery. Celery seed has tonic, diuretic and carminative properties. White-stalked celery was developed in Italy at the beginning of the eighteenth century.

Put celery seeds in soups, sauces, pickles and chutneys, and meat casseroles. Like basil, it has an affinity with tomatoes.

CHERVIL. Another member of the parsley family, *Anthriscus cerefolium* has leaves with a nice spicy flavour. It may be grown from seed in partial shade.

Used in traditional medicine as a blood cleanser, the leaves are excellent in salads, egg and cheese dishes and as a garnish for pork, veal and beef. They also go very well with many vegetables, including roots, beans and peas.

CHIVES. A relative of the onion, *Allium schoenoprasum* has a pleasant, mild onion taste and aroma. This hardy perennial is easy to grow and its thick clumps with their pretty mauve flowers soon make a good edging plant for the herb garden.

Use in biscuits and with cheese, eggs, fish and veal. The long green leaves are excellent as a garnish, and the flowers may also be used in this way.

CINNAMON. The curled brown sticks of *Cinnamomum zeylanicum* have a warm, sweet, aromatic flavour. The bark of the cinnamon tree was known in medieval England when it was still very expensive. The trees were not actively cultivated until the late eighteenth century, since until 1770 the monopoly was held by the Dutch traders, who preferred to use the wild trees. Cinnamon is a carminative, a stimulant and an astringent.

It is used in cakes and sweet dishes and in some meat dishes. Use pieces of whole cinnamon for savoury food and ground cinnamon for cakes. Buy ground cinnamon in small quantities since it deteriorates rapidly.

CITRUS FRUITS. *Citrus spp.* The Rutaceae family includes the lemon, C. *limonia*, the bitter orange, C. *aurantium*, and the sweet orange, C. *sinensis*, which are all used in cookery. Their sharp flavour is due to the presence of citric acid, and the sharpest are the bitter oranges. Citrus fruits, apart from supplying vitamins A, B and C, are tonic and carminative. They can help to reduce fever, nausea and thirst. The trees, which are thought of today as typically Mediterranean, were introduced into Europe by the Arabs in the twelfth century from the Middle and Far East.

The oily peel, or zest, is aromatic and flavoursome. Citrus juice is best made fresh when needed. Citrus rind and juice is used in soups, sauces, stuffings, marinades, salads and salad dressings, cakes and pastries. Lemon juice whitens and tenderizes the flesh of fish, seafood and pale meats. It is often used in jam-making to increase the pectin content and so aid setting.

Add grated lemon peel to poultry stuffings. Use grated orange peel to make orange butter which is delicious with grilled fish. Cumberland sauce, served with game, contains both orange and lemon peel. In traditional English cookery, citrus peel is an essential ingredient in fruit cakes, buns, mincemeat and Christmas puddings.

CLOVES. The dried buds of *Eugenia caryophyllus* have a sweetly pungent, aromatic flavour and are best bought whole since powdered cloves rapidly deteriorate. Clove oil is a powerful stumulant and carminative; soak cotton wool in clove oil and apply to an aching tooth to deaden the pain.

Cloves have been popular in English cookery since the Middle Ages. Use a few in soups and casseroles. Stud hams and pork joints. An onion studded with a few cloves is used to impart a special fragrance to stocks, soups, stews and sauces, in particular bread sauce. Apples are also improved by adding one or two cloves to the dish. Cloves are also used to flavour marinades, mulled wines, ale and cider cups.

CORIANDER. This member of the parsley family has leaves which are excellent as a garnish or in salads. They are strongly aromatic and should be used like parsley. The plant should be grown in good soil in full sunlight.

The seeds of *Coriandrum sativum* were found by archeologists on the floor of a late Bronze Age (c. 500 BC) hut at Minnis Bay, Kent. They represent the earliest record of a herb and spice which had probably been imported from the Mediterranean region. Coriander was widely used in English cookery until the Renaissance, when the more exotic spices began to arrive from the East.

Use the seeds – which are best bought whole – in basting sauces, breads, cakes, jellies and creams. Use the green leaf in herb butter, with beef, game, lamb, pork, ham and fish dishes, and as a garnish.

CUMIN. The seed of the cumin plant, *Cuminum cyminum* which, like coriander, is a member of the parsley family, was ground and used as a substitute for pepper by the Romans. It does not feature widely in English cookery, though the ground seed does appear in traditional recipes.

It should not be confused with the smaller and darker caraway seed, neither should it be substituted for it. It should always be used sparingly on account of its strong, pungent, aromatic flavour.

DILL. *Anethum graveolens* is a member of the parsley family that is used in traditional medicine for its calming and sleep-inducing properties. The light brown seeds were brought to Britain by the Romans and were very common in seventeenth-century England in sauces and pickles.

Use the seeds in bread and cakes. Use the leaf in salads and fish sauces, also with lamb and mutton, pork and ham, in cheese and pastry dishes and as a garnish.

FENNEL. *Foeniculum vulgare* is very like dill to look at, but the leaves have a characteristic taste of anise. Another herb of traditional medicine, an infusion of the leaves is good for sore or tired eyes. Fennel tea has a mild diuretic and laxative effect.

Add the leaves to salad and use as a garnish with fish, potatoes, eggs, lamb and mutton, offal, pork and ham, and in herb butter. Use the seeds in bread and fruit dishes.

GARLIC. The lily-like plant *Allium sativum* has a compound bulb which divides into 'cloves'. When buying make sure that the cloves are firm and not discoloured. Garlic has been used in medicines since ancient times. It is an aid to digestion, it stimulates the blood flow and lowers blood pressure. Garlic was once a popular flavouring in English cookery and then went almost completely out of fashion. In the late twentieth century it has become more widely used with the growing influence of modern continental cookery.

Joints of lamb are greatly improved by spiking with a few cloves of garlic before roasting. It also goes very well with dishes of game and offal. It will give a special fragrance and taste to sauces and gravies, but it should not be allowed to overcook.

GINGER. It is the swollen roots of *Zingiber officinale* that are used in cookery. Ginger is one of the earliest spices known in England where it has been used since the ninth century. It was a common article of medieval and Renaissance trade and was one of the spices used in an attempt to ward off plague.

The plant grows best in the tropics, and Jamaican ginger is considered to be of superior quality. In England, ginger has traditionally been used mainly in its dried and powdered or crystallized form, because of the difficulty in earlier centuries of transporting the root in fresh condition.

It is used in cakes, puddings, biscuits, jams and preserves, ginger beer and ginger wine. Powdered ginger is often served as a condiment with fresh melon.

HORSERADISH. The cylindrical white root of *Amoracia rusticana* may be purchased fresh, grated or dried and powdered. Grating your own horseradish will produce even more tears than chopping an onion! Horseradish is a stimulant, diuretic and antiseptic, richer in vitamin C than citrus fruits. It has been growing wild in England since the sixteenth century, and the root and leaves were originally used in traditional medicine.

Horseradish sauce is the classic accompaniment to roast beef, but it is also good with fish.

JUNIPER. The evergreen juniper tree, *Juniperus communis*, grows wild in England and is a member of the cupressus family. It prefers a sunny aspect and a chalky soil.

The strong flavour of the small, dark blue berries goes well with strong meats such as game. It also goes well with pork, bacon, roast lamb and veal. It makes an excellent spice for pointing up the taste of fruits such as apples.

LOVAGE. *Levisticium officinale* has leaves quite like celery. When put in bathwater, the leaves help to cleanse and deodorize the skin. The plant can be propagated by root division in the spring – you might know a friend who could supply you with a root – or grown from seed.

It is excellent in salads, but use sparingly until you are sure how to blend other flavours with its strong, celery-like taste.

MACE. This spice is the outer covering (aril) of the fruit of the nutmeg tree, *Myristica fragrans*, and its sweet, pungent fragrance is stronger than that of nutmeg. It dries to a dull yellow-brown colour and is sold in flat pieces known as 'blades'. One or two blades are usually enough for any dish. It is best bought in small quantities because it tends to deteriorate rapidly.

Popular in England since medieval times, the spice has been traditionally used in potted cheese and meats. Like nutmeg, mace can be used in both savoury and sweet dishes. Add a little pounded mace to potatoes or root vegetables.

MARJORAM. Sometimes called origanum, *Origanum majorana*, sweet marjoram, is related to the oregano of Italian cookery (*O. vulgare*).

Because of its spicy, aromatic taste it is excellent for use with meat and bland vegetables such as potato and marrow, cheese, eggs, fish, game, lamb and mutton, pork and ham, poultry, veal; and in biscuits, herb butter and pastry. Use the purple or pink flowers as a garnish.

MINT. Like the parsley family, the mint family offers a great selection of potherbs. Many kinds of mint are now available, most of which are hardy and grow vigorously. The most common is spearmint, *Mentha spicata*. Try to acquire two or more types since each one has its own special mint flavour and aroma.

Mint is the perfect herb for lamb and mutton because it neutralizes the taste of fat. It is also excellent in salads, biscuits, cheese and fruit dishes; as a garnish for fritters, potatoes and pies, and in wine or cider cups. Mint tea is a pleasant cooling drink and a very good digestive.

MUSTARD. English mustard is a bright yellow powder made from a blend of the powdered white and black seeds of the mustard plant, *Brassica juncea*, with a little wheat flour and turmeric. A blend of the seeds alone can be obtained.

Mustard develops its pungent qualities only after mixing with a cool liquid. Mix powdered mustard with water, lemon juice, vinegar, cider, beer or wine. For traditional English mustard, use 2 parts powder to 1 part liquid. Leave to stand for 15 minutes to allow the pungency to develop.

Use as a condiment with roast beef, pork, ham, bacon, sausages and meat pies. Mustard is also an ingredient in mustard sauce for herrings and an essential ingredient in piccalilli.

NASTURTIUM. *Tropaeolum majus* is an easily grown, trailing garden annual. The seed is a much neglected spice. The flowers, buds and leaves can also be used, but with caution since they all have a sharp, pungent flavour. The seeds may be used as a substitute for capers and also in salads.

NUTMEG. *Myristica fragrans*, a large tropical evergreen, was originally native to the Moluccas (Spice Islands), and the brown fruit has been known in England since the fourteenth century. It is best to purchase whole nutmegs and grate when required. Nutmeg is slightly poisonous so it should be used in moderation.

Traditionally added to English puddings, it is also good in pies, custards and cakes. Onion sauce and bread sauce should include some grated nutmeg. It goes well with egg dishes, green vegetables and dried pulses.

PARSLEY. If the English cook knows no other herb, parsley, *Petroselinum crispum*, at least will be familiar. However, it can be too familiar, frequently being the only and universal garnish. If you have never used anything but parsley as a herb garnish, get to know a few more herbs and experiment with them. You are in for some pleasant and exciting surprises. Curly-leaved parsley is the variety generally used for garnishes, but the flat-leaved variety has far more flavour. It is like coriander to look at, but it has its own distinctive taste.

Use with beef, eggs, fish, poultry and veal.

PENNYROYAL. *Mentha pulegium* is one of a number of ancient mints which have been largely replaced by varieties of spearmint (*M. spicata*). This little creeping plant is worth getting to know since its flavour is quite unique.

Use sparingly in soups and stuffings.

PEPPER. Known as the 'King of Spices', pepper is the powdered or ground form of the fruit (peppercorn) of the pepper plant, *Piper nigrum*. Black pepper is made from the dried unripe fruit, and white from the fruit when it is almost ripe. Peppercorns should be bought whole, as freshly ground pepper is superior to the ready bought powder. Generally, I choose to use black pepper and, in the recipes including pepper in this book, I have always used freshly ground black peppercorns.

Since ancient times pepper has been cultivated as a spice and condiment and has been an important item of international trade. From the Middle Ages, pepper formed the basis of the European spice trade.

ROSEMARY. *Rosmarinus officinalis* is a strongly aromatic plant which grows well in a pot in a sunny, well-drained position.

It is delicious sprinkled fresh on joints of lamb or even goat; with certain fish like halibut; with eggs, game, offal, pork and ham, poultry and veal. Use in basting sauces, cakes, fruit and wine cups. The blue flowers form an attractive garnish.

RUE. Still found in traditional herb gardens, rue (*Ruta graveolens*) was introduced by the Romans. It is used in herbal medicine as a stimulant.

Its leaves should be used sparingly because of their bitter taste, but it is an excellent foil to 'sweet' herbs.

SAFFRON. This spice is bought as the bright orange-red stigmas of the saffron crocus, *Crocus sativa*. The English name comes from the Arabic *za'faran*, yellow. Steep a pinch in a cup of hot water or milk to release the characteristic colour, flavour and aroma. It cannot be substituted for or by turmeric. Saffron is the world's most expensive spice and no more than a pinch is ever necessary in any recipe.

It was used by the Romans in medicine, as a spice and as a dye, and was in wide use in England up to the Renaissance. Since the Middle Ages it had been cultivated around the Essex town of Saffron Walden, whose arms still include three saffron crocuses.

Today it is added to cake and bun mixtures in Devon and Cornwall, but its use in other forms of cookery has virtually died out in England.

SAGE. *Salvia officinalis* was originally a medicinal herb introduced by the Romans as a tonic and cure-all. It is nowadays one of the best known of the stuffing herbs. Try it in other situations, but beware of its powerful aromatic properties which are reminiscent of camphor. It is easy to grow in a sunny, well-drained position. Sage leaves make a good restorative tea, and this liquid is also good for the skin and for conditioning the hair.

Sprinkle fresh on roast pork or rabbit. Use with cheese, game, lamb and mutton, offal and poultry, in pastry and as a garnish. Save the blue or red flowers for use as a garnish.

SAVORY. *Satureja hortensis* is another member of the mint family which was introduced by the Romans, and its use in cookery predates that of sage. Use sparingly on account of its bitter taste.

It is very good with beans, other legumes, eggs and lamb dishes.

SORREL

'Out nettle, in dock!'

Sorrel, as its specific name, *Rumex acetosa*, shows, is an acid dock and belongs to the same family as rhubarb. Sorrel leaves were a popular flavouring herb in medieval England, but today they are hardly used at all. They are easy to grow and have a refreshing, vinegary taste.

Sorrel is excellent in stuffings and salads. Cook lightly and serve with veal, pork and fish, or in soups and bean dishes. It is the basis of the old English sour green sauces which can accompany pork, venison, duck and goose.

TARRAGON. *Artemesia dracunculus* is considered by some to be one of the great potherbs, like parsley, though it is traditionally a typically French, rather than an English, herb. The hay-like aroma of tarragon can be substituted by rue.

Use with cheese, eggs, fish, lamb and mutton, offal, pork and ham, poultry and veal; in pastry and as a garnish.

THYME. It is a good idea to cultivate your own garden thyme since the wild thymes of England are less flavoursome. As with mint, many varieties are obtainable, so it should be possible to grow more than one for your own use. The warm, pungent flavour of *Thymus vulgaris* is an essential ingredient in a 'bunch of sweet herbs'.

It is excellent with lamb, pork, veal, poultry, game, beef, cheese, eggs, fish, offal; and in basting sauces, biscuits, bread, herb butter and pastry. Use the purple flowers as a garnish.

TURMERIC. *Curcuma domestica* is the dried and powdered underground stem of a tropical, ginger-like plant. The bright yellow powder should be bought in small quantities as it deteriorates quickly. Turmeric is an effective yellow dye which can be removed by washing. In cookery it cannot be substituted for or by saffron.

It is an essential ingredient in piccalilli and some mustard pickles, but should be used sparingly on account of its strong, bitter taste.

WATERCRESS. *Nasturtium officinale* is related to the peppery garden nasturtium and is one of the few aquatic herbs. It is rich in iron and vitamin C and its medicinal properties have been known since ancient times. It prefers to grow in the shallow, sandy bed of a running stream so it is not a herb that can be grown in most gardens.

Always use it fresh in salads, as a garnish or as an ingredient in soups.

# Basic Wholefood Ingredients

To obtain the best results from the recipes in this book, try to use additive-free, wholefood ingredients wherever possible. Avoid refined, additive-adulterated or processed foods.

ALE, BEER AND CIDER. It is still possible to obtain 'real' versions of these drinks, due largely to pressure from people who want to preserve traditional crafts and tastes. Your local health food shop or conservation group will be able to help you if you have any difficulty.

EGGS. Free-range eggs are slightly more expensive than those laid by battery hens. They are, however, additive-free and have not been produced by a bird under stress. Free-range birds are at liberty to graze and scratch about for their natural foods, which results in a superior egg. Many farms have changed to free-range and your health food shop should be able to supply them. Their increasing popularity has also led to some supermarkets stocking them, too.

FATS. The latest four-lettered word sends shivers down many spines, yet there is nothing frightening about fats. They are natural foods and should form part of a well-balanced diet. Animal fats contain cholesterol which is suspected of causing harmful effects when consumed in large quantities by those who do little physical exercise or who overeat. Because these fats are easily retained by the body but are not easy to burn up as energy, they should be used in moderation and with common sense. A range of natural fats which have specific uses in traditional cookery is suggested in this book.

*Butter* is a good, wholesome food made from cream, and usually only contains the additive of salt. It may be used in combination with other cooking fats, but should not be overheated since it will easily burn.

*Lard* is rendered and clarified pork fat. Use it in moderation.

*Dripping* is the fat from cooked animals and birds. It is an excellent cooking medium since it also contains specific flavours and ingredients from basting, garnishing, etc. It was once very popular spread on hot toast instead of butter. Keep it in a cool place like other fats, and do not allow it to become too old.

*Suet* is solid animal fat which has been finely shredded. Commercial suet has undergone a process of purification, but your local butcher should be able to supply unprocessed suet. It is a common myth that suet makes for heavy, indigestible food. This is more likely to be due to a poor combination of ingredients and bad cooking. All animal fats solidify on cooling and for this reason recipes which include suet are designed to be eaten hot.

*Cooking oils* are processed from vegetable or other ingredients, but many varieties claim to be additive free. *Margarine* is not considered a wholefood, because it includes certain additives.

FLOUR. The flour specified in this book is 100 per cent wholemeal flour which contains bran, the essential fibre needed for proper digestion and the prevention of digestive disorders. There are now many brands in the shops, and each has its own characteristics. If you get to know your flour you will have better results when making bread, pastry or cakes. Made with wholemeal flour, they will have more flavour and are better for you.

MEAT. The nutritional advice of this book, in line with modern thinking, is to reduce the consumption of animal protein to once or twice a week.

As a 1984 study by the Vegetarian Society has shown, most butchers and supermarkets are unable to give details about drug residues, hormones and growth-producers present in their meat. However, there are now butchers up and down the country who are able to deliver frozen, additive-free meat. If there is no such butcher in your area, a group could get together to make a bulk purchase (usually a minimum of 30–40 lb). I quote from the details supplied by F.A. and J. Jones of Red House Farm, North Scarle, Lincoln:

We feed traditional foods and turn our beasts out to graze in spring, summer and autumn. We bed all our animals on straw.

We hang all our beef fourteen days to mature naturally in the traditional manner.

We do not feed urea, processed manure, antibiotics, arsenicals, growth promoters. We do not inject with steroids prior to slaughter. We do not use TVP in our sausages and pies.

We do not use artificial flavourings, preservatives or colourings in any of our products.

Butchers such as F. A. and J. Jones are only too pleased to supply detailed information about their products, including the cost and despatch details.

All game is of course additive-free. It is also possible to obtain free-range and additive-free poultry.

STOCK. The old habit of having a stockpot and making vegetable, meat or fish stock has almost died out among English cooks under the constant pressure to save time and labour. In spite of the galaxy of labour-saving devices installed in most homes, the stock cube prevails and all those useful odds and ends of food end up in the rubbish bin. A quick look at the ingredients of a cube may convince you that it contains things which you may not want to eat.

The refrigerator, and especially the freezer, are the stockmaker's blessing. Next time you have a carcase or some food scraps handy, make up a stock and simmer it for some time so that it is rich and concentrated; then just freeze it in little cubes in an ice tray for use when required.

SUGAR. The sugar suggested in this book is soft brown, additive-free sugar which has passed through few processes and still retains some of its original flavour and aroma. Honey may be substituted whenever sugar is mentioned in any of the recipes; the amount to use is discretionary.

Sugar should be regarded more as a spice than as a food and consequently used in moderation.

VEGETABLES AND FRUIT. You cannot avoid food additives and other polluting chemicals simply by going vegetarian. Most commercially produced fruit and vegetables receive doses of pesticide, fungicide and weedkiller along with other specific chemicals used for individual crops, and are grown with artificial fertilizers. It is worthwhile, therefore, either to grow your own with the aid of organic compost, or to purchase 'organically grown' fruit and vegetables through your local supplier. Patrick Holden, who has been farming organically in West Wales for fifteen years, supplies countrywide. There are now many farmers like him, supplying the increasing public demand for additive-free food.

WINE AND VINEGAR. Both these important ingredients in cookery have, like ale and cider, come under the threat of chemical additives. Try to obtain wine and vinegar which are still being made in the traditional manner. Suppliers will know of a demand only if the product is asked for.

# Weights, Measures & Oven Temperatures

The English cook of the past tended to use whatever was to hand and would modify a recipe accordingly. In the same spirit, measuring was usually carried out by the use and judgement of hand and eye.

In this book simple weights and measures are provided in both imperial and metric, but in most cases they may be varied according to taste and necessity. Measurements are most critical in the baking recipes, where a deviation could result in disappointment. Use the recipes as starting points for your own experiments.

The cup measure in this book is one which holds 8 fl oz (225 ml) water and 4 oz (100 g) flour.

The teaspoon holds approximately ⅙ fl oz (5 ml) and the tablespoon holds approximately ½ fl oz (15 ml).

The recipes are sufficient for four to six people, unless otherwise stated.

## CONVERSION TABLES

All these conversions are close approximations. Never mix imperial and metric measurements in a recipe.

| WEIGHT | | | | | | | | | |
|---|---|---|---|---|---|---|---|---|---|
| oz | ½ | 1 | 1½ | 2 | 3 | 4 | 4½ | 5 | 6 |
| g | 14 | 28 | 42 | 60 | 85 | 110 | 125 | 140 | 170 |
| oz | 7 | 8 | 9 | 10 | 12 | 1lb | 2lb | 3lb | |
| g | 200 | 225 | 250 | 275 | 340 | 450 | 900 | 1030 (1·3 kg) | |

## VOLUME

| fl oz | 2 | 3 | 5(¼ pt) | 10 (½pt) | 15 (¾pt) | 20 (1 pt) |
|---|---|---|---|---|---|---|
| ml | 55 | 85 | 140 | 285 | 425 | 570 |
| pt | 1¾ | 2 | | | | |
| litres | 1 | 1·1 | | | | |

## OVEN TEMPERATURES

| Mark | 1 | 2 | 3 | 4 | 5 | 6 | 7 | 8 | 9 |
|---|---|---|---|---|---|---|---|---|---|
| °F | 275 | 300 | 325 | 350 | 375 | 400 | 425 | 450 | 475 |
| °C | 140 | 150 | 170 | 180 | 190 | 200 | 220 | 230 | 240 |

# Soups, Broths & Pottages

You must observe in all broths and soups, that one thing does not taste more than another, but that the taste be equal, and that it has a fine agreeable relish, according to what you may design for it; and you must be sure, that all the greens and herbs you put in are clean washed and picked.

*Mrs Cole's Cookery, 1791*

The general adoption of the fork late in the seventeenth century had an effect on the thick medieval pottage. Now it was no longer necessary to eat chopped meat or fish as a spoonmeat in pottage. The broth could be served separately and eaten with a spoon, and the meat or fish eaten later with a knife and fork.

About this time, simple broths and running porridges or pottages became known in France as *soupe*, and thin pottage became fashionable among the English gentry under the title of 'soup'. From the early eighteenth century the soup ceased to be substantial like a pottage and became an appetizer. By the nineteenth century this had become the established pattern of dishes, with soup being served before the main dish.

In the poorer households, it was generally agreed sensible to use up the scraps and left-overs to create this most adaptable of dishes – a custom adopted nowadays by cooks everywhere. In *The Complete Cottage Cookery* of 1859, for example, Esther Copley relates one of the classic soup stories. I have come across this one in India and in Spain, with only slight changes in the list of ingredients. Here, the effect is tempered with a spoonful of Victorian ethics.

The story is told by a widow to another lady. When she was first married, she confides, she generally had flint soup for dinner once a week. The second lady, eyebrows raised and agog for information, has never heard of such a soup, and asks what could it be good for? The widow replies,

I will tell you. The first Saturday after we were married, my husband brought home his wages. 'Now, Mary,' said he, 'I must lay by for you – rent – for firing and for clothing; and here is the remainder, for you to make the best of for our supply through the week.' I got things very comfortably and, as I thought, very frugally, but by the next Friday evening, after supper, I had to say to my husband, 'What must we do? The money is all gone and we have nothing in the house for tomorrow's dinner. I am sure I have made it go as far as I could.'

My husband was very kind, he found no fault, but said we could have flint soup for dinner. He asked if there was any bread in the house and a little oatmeal or flour, and plenty of herbs in the garden? Then he washed a couple of flints very clean and set them on with some water and onions, and a carrot or two. When the roots were tender he put in the meal and some pepper and salt, parsley and thyme and the piece of stale bread and I assure you we had a good dinner.

At this point the other lady inquires as to the use of the flints. Why not leave them out and call it herb porridge?

That is what I could not understand at first. Well, next Saturday matters were much the same, so we contentedly dined on flint soup. In the course of the following week, having picked some bones of meat, I was going to throw them away when the thought struck me, that if they were chopped up and put in the soup they would give at least as much goodness as the flints. My husband thought so too. So we tried, and found they greatly improved the soup, and from that time we never wasted a bone. In the course of a few weeks we found the money held out for Saturday's dinner, and even allowed a trifle to lay by. Then my husband told me the real use of the flints in the soup.

'There are two things which I have always resolved against: debt and waste. So from the day I took to providing for myself, I determined always to keep bread in the house and to live on bread and water rather than run into debt. But instead of eating dry bread and drinking cold water, I set myself to make it into soup; for I thought if I boiled down the flints, which could not enrich the liquor, it might sharpen my wits to make the best use of anything that I could. I can truly say that making flint soup has taught me to turn to good account many things that are often thrown away as if they were worthless stones.'

# CRAB SOUP

| | |
|---|---|
| 1¾ pt (1 litre) chicken stock | ½ teaspoon salt |
| 3 oz (85 g) whole grain wheat | freshly ground pepper |
| | ¼ teaspoon grated nutmeg |
| | 1 medium crab, cooked |
| 1¾ pt (1 litre) milk | ¼ pt (140 ml) double cream |

Put the chicken stock and wheat in a large saucepan and bring to the boil. Stir well and simmer for 10 minutes. Add the milk and seasoning and bring back to the boil. Simmer until the wheat is soft. Take the flesh from the crab. Chop the pale meat and pound the dark. Add to the soup and check the seasoning. Stir in the cream gently and do not allow the soup to boil. Serve garnished with chopped herbs.

*See also the recipe for:*
Cheese Pottage

# MUSSEL SOUP

| | |
|---|---|
| 2 pt (1·1 litres) mussels, washed and scraped | 1 small parsnip, peeled and sliced |
| 2 pt (1.1 litres) water | 1 leek, chopped |
| 12 almonds | 4 oz (110 g) mushrooms, chopped |
| 12 prawns, shelled | small bunch of sweet herbs |
| 2 tablespoons butter *or* cooking oil | 1 tablespoon chopped parsley |
| 1 small onion, chopped | freshly grated nutmeg |
| 1 carrot, peeled and sliced | freshly ground pepper |
| | salt to taste |

Discard any mussels that are not tightly shut or that do not shut when tapped. Put in a saucepan with the water. Cover and boil for 5 minutes or until the shells open. Throw away any that have not opened. Strain off and keep the liquid. Leave the mussels until cool enough to handle, then remove them from their shells. Blanch the almonds in boiling water, skin and pound. Pound the prawns and mix with the almonds. Heat the butter or oil in a soup pan and fry the onion until transparent. Add the carrot and parsnip and fry for 2 minutes. Add the leek, mushrooms, prawn mixture and mussels. Make the mussel liquid up to 2 pt (1·1 litres) with a little stock or water and pour into the soup pan. Add the herbs and seasoning. Cook on a gentle heat for 10 minutes or until the roots are tender. Serve with small squares of fried bread.

## PRAWN SOUP

| | |
|---|---|
| 1 pt (570 ml) prawns | 4 cloves |
| 2 tablespoons butter *or* cooking oil | freshly ground pepper |
| 1 small onion, chopped | 1 teaspoon thyme |
| 1 cup finely chopped vegetables | 1 anchovy |
| ½ teaspoon mace | 2 pt (1·1 litres) hot water |

Shell the prawns. Heat the butter in a soup pan and gently fry the onion until transparent. Add the prawns and chopped vegetables and turn them in the butter. Add the spices. Pound the thyme with the anchovy and add to the pan with the hot water. Simmer gently for 30 minutes.

## EEL SOUP

| | |
|---|---|
| 2 tablespoons butter *or* cooking oil | 1 blade of mace |
| 1 small onion, chopped | 4 peppercorns |
| 1 lb (450 g) eels, cut in pieces | small bunch of sweet herbs |
| 1 crust of bread, broken in pieces | 2 pt (1·1 litres) hot water |

Heat the butter in a soup pan and gently fry the onion until transparent. Add the eels, bread, spices and herbs. Pour the hot water over them. Cover and simmer until the eel is tender and the flesh can easily be removed from the bone. Remove the bone and serve the soup with lightly toasted bread.

## WHITE FISH SOUP

| | |
|---|---|
| 1 lb (450 g) cod *or* other white fish | ¼ pt (140 ml) milk |
| 1 medium onion, chopped | 1 teaspoon chopped fennel |
| 1 stick celery, sliced | 1 teaspoon chopped lovage |
| 2 pt (1·1 litres) water | 1 tablespoon chopped parsley |
| ¼ pt (140 ml) white wine | finely grated rind of ½ lemon |
| 1 tablespoon flour | freshly ground pepper |
| | salt |

Put the fish, onion and celery into a saucepan and add the water. Bring to the boil and simmer for 15 minutes or until the fish is just cooked. Take the fish from the pan, remove the skin and bones and return these to the pan. Continue simmering for a further 30 minutes. Strain, and return the stock to the pan. Add the wine. Cut the fish into chunks and add to the pan. Blend the flour with ½ cup of cold water, taking care that there are no lumps. Stir in a little of the hot soup, blend well and add this mixture to the soup in the pan. Bring to the boil, stirring constantly. Add the milk, herbs, lemon peel and seasoning to taste.

## PIKE IN BROTH

In the fourteenth century verjuice, a sour juice made from unripe grapes or apples, would have been added to this broth. Large freshwater fish were frequently stewed in wine and verjuice with oranges, dates and spices to make a nourishing and tasty fish broth.

| | |
|---|---|
| 1 pike, carp *or* other freshwater fish | 1 blade of mace |
| 1 tablespoon currants *or* sultanas | 1 tablespoon cider vinegar *or* wine |
| 1 tablespoon prunes | vinegar |
| 4 oz (110 g) peeled and cored | 2 pt (1·1 litres) water |
| cooking apples *or* crab apples | freshly ground pepper |
| small bunch of sweet herbs | salt |

Cut the fish in pieces and put in a soup pan. Add the currants, prunes, apples, herbs, mace and vinegar. Pour the water into the pan and bring to the boil. Cook on a gentle heat for 15 minutes. Add pepper and salt to taste. Continue cooking until the fish is tender. Serve the fish in a little of its broth or break off the flesh from the bones and serve as a rich fish broth with toasted bread.

## HADDOCK SOUP WITH FORCEMEAT BALLS

| | |
|---|---|
| 3 fresh *or* smoked haddock | 1 pt (570 ml) prawns, shelled |
| ½ teaspoon chilli powder *or* | 1 tablespoon chopped parsley |
| cayenne pepper | 1 cup breadcrumbs |
| ½ teaspoon powdered mace | 1 egg, beaten |
| 2½ pt (1·4 litres) water | 1 tablespoon flour |

Put the fish in a soup pan and sprinkle with chilli powder and mace. Cover with water and bring to the boil. Cook on a gentle heat until the fish is tender. Remove one of the fish, skin and take the flesh from the bones. Allow the other two fish to go on cooking. Pound the flesh in a bowl with the prawns, parsley, breadcrumbs and egg. Make up the mixture into little balls. Strain off the broth from the other two haddock. Blend the flour with ½ cup cold water, making sure there are no lumps. Add to the fish broth. Put in the forcemeat balls and turn up the heat before serving.

# CREAMED PORK POTTAGE

While ordinary folk ate their pease pottage or green porray, the gentry enjoyed rich spicy meat and fish pottages introduced from Norman France. The great Anglo–Norman pottages took their form not from the meat or fish they contained, but from the sauce in which those ingredients were cooked. 'Civey' might include pieces of hare, rabbit or duck on a meat day, or tench, sole or oysters on a fasting day; its principal feature, however, was the use of onions to flavour the stock in which the pieces of meat or fish were stewed. Such a pottage was thickened with bread and laced with pepper and other spices.

In the later medieval period, pottage remained in favour at every level of society. Bread, pottage and ale were the three principal items of diet. Andrew Boorde noted in his *Dyetary of Helth* in 1542 that pottage was more popular in Britain than anywhere else in Europe. The ingredients were many and varied, but the result was always a semi-liquid spoonmeat. Several forms of cereal pottage evolved, based on the breadcorn (i.e. the wheat, barley or oats) of the region.

To flavour these pottages, the housewife grew or gathered as many as fifty different herbs, including dandelion, leeks, garlic and several aromatics such as sage and thyme. This one is adapted from a thick medieval broth known as *charlet*. On special occasions, powdered ginger and sugar would be added and each serving was topped with grated nutmeg or cinnamon.

| | |
|---|---|
| 2 tablespoons butter *or* cooking oil | 2 eggs, beaten |
| 1 small onion, chopped | pinch of saffron |
| 8 oz (225 g) lean pork, shredded | freshly ground pepper |
| ½ pt (285 ml) milk | salt |
| 1½ pt (850 ml) stock *or* water | 1 tablespoon chopped fresh parsley |

Heat the butter in a soup pan and fry the onion until transparent. Add the pork and turn it in the butter for 5 minutes. Pour the milk and stock into the pan. Stir in the eggs and saffron. Bring to the boil and simmer gently for 30 minutes. Add pepper and salt to taste. Serve garnished with chopped fresh herbs.

# MEAT POTTAGE

The successor of the medieval 'long worts de char' was a meat pottage known in the sixteenth and seventeenth centuries as 'Bukkenade'. The everyday vehicle for any pieces of boiled meat which may have been available, it became one of the national dishes of the time, called by the French 'pottage in the English style'. Here is a version from the sixteenth century.

| | |
|---|---|
| 8 oz–1 lb (225–450 g) meat pieces (veal, kid, chicken or rabbit) | 1 tablespoon currants *or* sultanas |
| ½ teaspoon powdered mace | 1 tablespoon vinegar |
| 2 cloves | 2 egg yolks, beaten |
| 2 peppercorns | 2 pt (1·1 litres) water |
| 1 tablespoon ground almonds | salt |

Put the meat pieces in a soup pan. Sprinkle with the spices, ground almonds and currants. Cover with the vinegar and egg yolks. Pour the water into the pan and bring to the boil. After 30 minutes add salt to taste. Cook the soup on a gentle heat until it begins to thicken and the meat is tender.

# GIBLET SOUP

| | |
|---|---|
| rabbit *or* chicken giblets | ½ teaspoon marjoram |
| 2 pt (1·1 litres) stock | 1 glass red wine *or* port |
| 2 tablespoons chopped parsley | freshly ground pepper |
| 1 tablespoon chopped chives | salt |
| 1 teaspoon pennyroyal | 1 tablespoon flour |

Put the giblets in a soup pan and cover with the stock. Boil gently until the giblets are tender. Remove them, and pound or chop fine. Put back in the stock. Add the herbs, wine, pepper and salt to taste. Mix the flour with a little cold water in a cup, making sure there are no lumps. Add a little hot stock and pour the mixture into the soup pan. Simmer gently for 10 minutes, then serve.

# CHICKEN BROTH

'No broth, no ball; no ball, no beef' was a Georgian saying referring to the Elizabethan practice of beginning the main meal with broth. After that came a suet pudding, then the meat course.

In the Middle Ages the broth below was known as *gravey*. Any other cheap meat such as rabbit or eel could be used instead of or in addition to the chicken. *Gravey* was often enforced with hard-boiled egg yolks and grated cheese, when it was called *gravey enforced*.

| | |
|---|---|
| 8 oz (225 g) boned chicken, shredded | 1 teaspoon salt |
| 2 pt (1·1 litres) stock *or* water | 1 teaspoon sugar |
| 2 tablespoons ground almonds | ½ teaspoon ground ginger |
| freshly ground pepper | pinch of grated nutmeg |
| | 1 tablespoon chopped parsley |

Put the chicken in a soup pan and cover with the stock. Add the ground almonds, pepper and salt and cook on a gentle heat for 30 minutes. Add the rest of the seasoning before serving, garnished with parsley.

# HARE SOUP

| | |
|---|---|
| 1 hare *or* rabbit, skinned and trimmed | 12 oz (340 g) lean ham *or* bacon, diced |
| 2 onions, chopped | 2–3 pt (1·1–1·7 litres) stock |
| bunch of sweet herbs | ¼ teaspoon chilli powder *or* cayenne pepper |
| a few bay leaves | 1 teaspoon salt |
| 2 blades of mace | port or red wine |
| 6 cloves | (optional) |
| 6 peppercorns | |

Cut the hare in pieces. Put it in a large soup pan. Add the onion, herbs, spices and ham. Cover with stock and season with chilli and salt to taste. Bring to the boil and cook on a gentle heat until the meat is tender. Take the meat pieces from the pan and remove the meat from the bones. Put the meat back in the pan. This soup will benefit from the addition of a little port or red wine if you have some available.

# PULSE POTTAGE

Meat pottages changed in both flavour and texture between the Tudor period (1485–1603) and the end of the eighteenth century. Cereal pottages remained static, probably because they were eaten by humble folk. They tended to be breakfast or supper dishes – pottage for breakfast was common in all classes until late in the seventeenth century. Pottage got a bad name, by association, when it was used in institutions to feed the poor.

In the recipe below, cereals such as wheat and barley may be substituted for the dried pulses.

| | |
|---|---|
| 1 tablespoon chick peas | 1 tablespoon chopped coriander leaf |
| 1 tablespoon lentils | ½ tablespoon chopped dill leaf |
| 1 tablespoon dried peas *or* beans | ½ tablespoon chopped fennel leaf |
| 2 pt (1·1 litres) water | 1 teaspoon marjoram |
| 1 leek, chopped | 1 teaspoon chopped lovage |
| 1 tablespoon chopped beet tops | freshly ground pepper |
| ½ cup chopped cabbage | 1 teaspoon salt |

Soak the dried pulses in water overnight. Next day boil them in fresh water for 30 minutes, then discard the water. Add 2 pt (1·1 litres) fresh water and simmer. When the pulses are almost tender, add the chopped vegetables, herbs, pepper and salt. Cook together until the vegetables are tender.

# BEAN SOUP

| | |
|---|---|
| 8 oz (225 g) dried beans | 4 tablespoons butter *or* cooking oil |
| 1 onion, chopped | 2½ pt (1·4 litres) stock |
| 2 carrots, sliced and chopped | freshly ground pepper |
| 2 leeks, sliced | salt |
| 8 oz (225 g) tomatoes, chopped | chopped parsley *or* watercress |

Soak the beans in water the day before they are needed. Next morning change the water. Boil the beans in fresh water until they are tender. Drain. Meanwhile prepare the vegetables. Heat the butter in a soup pan and fry the onion until transparent. Add the vegetables and fry gently for 5 minutes. Pour the stock over them and cook until the vegetables are tender. Add the cooked beans, salt and pepper to taste. Serve garnished with chopped herbs.

# CARROT SOUP

| | |
|---|---|
| 2 tablespoons butter *or* cooking oil | 1 teaspoon salt |
| 2 onions, chopped | 1 tablespoon flour |
| 1½ lb (680 g) carrots, grated | ¼ teaspoon chilli powder *or* cayenne pepper |
| 2½ pt (1·4 litres) stock | 1 tablespoon chopped parsley |
| freshly ground pepper | 1 tablespoon chopped chervil |

Heat the butter in a soup pan and gently fry the onion until transparent. Add the carrots and stock. Season with pepper and salt to taste. Bring to the boil and simmer gently for 30 minutes. Rub the soup through a sieve or put it in a blender. Return to the pan. Mix the flour with the chilli powder in a cup and stir in a little cold water. Add to this paste some of the warm soup. Mix well and return to the pan. Simmer for 10 minutes. Garnish with herbs and serve with squares of fried bread.

# CAULIFLOWER SOUP

| | |
|---|---|
| 1 cauliflower | freshly ground pepper |
| 2 tablespoons butter *or* cooking oil | salt |
| 1 onion, chopped | 4 tablespoons yogurt |
| 2 pt (1·1 litres) stock | chopped chervil |

Wash the cauliflower and chop into small sprigs. Heat the butter and gently fry the onion until transparent. Add the cauliflower and turn until it is well covered with butter. Add the stock and simmer until the cauliflower is tender. Rub the soup through a sieve or put it in a blender. Return to the pan. Add pepper and salt to taste and stir in the yogurt. Gently reheat the soup. Serve garnished with the chopped chervil.

# CHESTNUT SOUP

This soup is excellent with pigeons and makes a very good broth to cook them in.

| | |
|---|---|
| 2 lb (900 g) chestnuts | 4 cloves |
| 2½ pt (1·4 litres) stock | 2 blades of mace |
| 2–4 slices ham, diced | bunch of sweet herbs |
| 8 oz (225 g) lean cooked meat, diced | freshly ground pepper |
| 1 onion, chopped | salt |

Roast the chestnuts in the oven or over a fire until they pop, then peel them. Put in a soup pan with the stock and boil gently for 30 minutes. Remove the chestnuts and mash them. Return to the pan. Add the ham, chopped meat, onion, spices, herbs, pepper and salt to taste. Simmer gently for 10 minutes. Serve hot with toasted bread.

## FASTING HERB SOUP

In former times many periods of the year were ordained by the Church as 'fasting', during which the eating of any kind of meat was not permitted. Thus one could eat one's fill while still 'fasting'. Today people generally fast for its beneficial effects in cleansing and resting the system. This is a nourishing light soup to follow a modest fast. For a more substantial soup, add partly cooked dried peas or beans and cook together with the vegetables.

| | |
|---|---|
| 1 tablespoon butter *or* cooking oil | 1 slice bread, crumbled |
| 1 onion, chopped | ½ teaspoon powdered mace |
| 2 sticks celery, chopped | freshly ground pepper |
| 1 cup chopped spinach | salt |
| 1 cup chopped lettuce | 2 egg yolks, beaten |
| 2 tablespoons chopped parsley | 1 tablespoon vinegar |
| 2 pt (1·1 litres) hot water | 1 tablespoon chopped watercress |

Heat the butter in a soup pan and fry the onion until transparent. Add the celery, spinach, lettuce and parsley and turn in the butter for 2 minutes. Pour the water into the pan. Add the bread, mace and pepper and salt to taste. Stir together and simmer gently for 30 minutes. Remove from the heat. Stir in the egg yolks and vinegar. Serve garnished with watercress.

## HERB SOUP

Now leeks are in season, for pottage full good,
and spareth the milchcow, and purgeth the blood.
These having with peason, for pottage in Lent,
thou sparest both oatmeal and bread to be spent.

Leeks were brought to England by the Romans and later became a popular food for Lent. The Middle English word *porray* (probably derived from the Latin *porrum*, a leek) was first applied to thick leek soups. Later the word came to mean any thick pottage of greenstuff. Eaten by rich and poor, they were the great standby of country folk. Beet leaves were another favourite, as were other large-leaved herbs such as orache, clary, mallow, dock,

borage and bugloss. Seasoning was provided by aromatic potherbs –
parsley, sage, thyme, mint, fennel and violet. Here is a simple herb soup
using leeks. More flavour may be added by including pinches of aromatic
herbs such as marjoram, basil and thyme. As a restorative for a hungry
patient, substitute for the vegetable stock chicken stock with a little
shredded chicken.

| | |
|---|---|
| 2 pt (1·1 litres) vegetable stock *or* water | 2 tablespoons chopped chervil |
| 2–4 leeks, chopped | 2 tablespoons chopped borage |
| 1 cup chopped celery | freshly ground pepper |
| 1 cup chopped spinach | salt |
| 2 tablespoons chopped sorrel | shredded lettuce |

Boil up the stock gently with the leeks and celery for 10 minutes. Add the
chopped herbs specified, or any others that you can get hold of. Boil gently
for a further 5 minutes. Add pepper and salt to taste. Serve with shredded
lettuce and lightly toasted bread.

## ONION SOUP

Onion skin very thin,
Mild winter coming in;
Onion skin thick and tough,
Winter coming cold and rough.

| | |
|---|---|
| 4 oz (110 g) lean ham, diced | 1 carrot, sliced |
| 1 cup lean meat, diced | bunch of sweet herbs |
| 2 onions, chopped | 3 allspice berries |
| 1 stalk celery, chopped | 3 pts (1·7 litres) water |
| 1 leek, chopped | freshly ground pepper |
| 1 cup chopped turnip *or* swede *or* parsnip | salt |
| | 12 small button onions *or* shallots |

Put the meat in a soup pan with the vegetables, herbs, allspice and 1 pt
(570 ml) of the water. Bring to the boil and simmer gently for 30 minutes.
Pour on 2 pints (1·1 litres) of hot water and season with pepper and salt to
taste. Add the button onions and boil gently until they are tender. Serve
with lightly toasted bread.

# PEA SOUP

Once the Industrial Revolution got under way, large towns and cities came to experience a thick greenish fog around riverside areas during the winter months which was quickly named 'pea soup'. This deadly mixture of sulphurous coal fumes and winter fog was aptly named. Traditionally, pea soup is green, though there are many modern variations that include other vegetables which can make the soup more of an orange or yellow colour.

| | |
|---|---|
| 2 lb (900 g) fresh peas *or* frozen peas | 1 teaspoon salt |
| | 2 tablespoons chopped parsley |
| 2 pt (1·1 litres) water | 1 tablespoon chopped mint |
| 2 tablespoons butter *or* cooking oil | 2 tablespoons chopped beet leaves |
| 2 anchovies (optional) | 1 tablespoon chopped spinach |
| ½ teaspoon freshly ground pepper | 1 teaspoon sugar |

Boil the peas in the water until tender and scrape the mixture through a coarse sieve or put in a blender. Put the butter into a large pan and heat gently. Add the anchovies, pepper, salt, parsley and other herbs. Turn them in the hot butter until they are well covered. Add the peas and cook until the greens are tender. Add the sugar just before serving.

# PEASE POTTAGE (DRIED PEA SOUP)

Peas pudding hot, peas pudding cold;
Peas pudding in the pot, nine days old!

Pease pottage was the national dish of Tudor and Stuart England. It became more and more a food of poorer folk during the eighteenth century and was no longer a national dish by the end of the century. Today it has survived in the north in a thicker form as peas pudding, traditionally served with ham or pork.

| | |
|---|---|
| 2 cups dried peas | 2 carrots, chopped |
| 1 ham bone *or* bacon bone | a few sage leaves |
| 2 pt (1·1 litres) water | a few mint leaves |
| 1 onion, chopped | freshly ground pepper |

Wash and soak the dried peas in water the day before they are needed. Next day change the water and continue soaking. Put the ham bone in a soup pan with the 2 pt (1·1 litres) of water and cook over a gentle heat for 30 minutes. Skim off any fat. Add the onion and carrot and continue cooking. Strain the peas and add to the pot. Add the herbs and pepper and continue cooking until the peas are soft, adding more water during the cooking if necessary. Serve with fried bread and a little vinegar to point up the flavour.

## LENTIL SOUP WITH MUSSELS

This soup was brought to England by Roman settlers living in fortified towns near the coast.

| | |
|---|---|
| 1 cup lentils | a few mint leaves |
| 2 pt (1·1 litres) water | 1 teaspoon rue |
| 2 bay leaves | 1 tablespoon vinegar |
| ½ teaspoon peppercorns | 1 teaspoon honey |
| ½ teaspoon cumin seeds | 1½ teaspoons salt |
| ½ teaspoon coriander seeds | 1½ cups boiled mussels |

Wash the lentils and put in a pan with the measured water. Allow to cook on a gentle heat until soft, skimming off the white scum that forms during cooking. Meanwhile pound the peppercorns, cumin and coriander seeds with the herbs. Moisten with a few drops of vinegar. Add the honey and salt, and stir the mixture into the cooked lentils. Add the mussels and cook together over a gentle heat for 15 minutes, adding more water if necessary. Stir in the rest of the vinegar.

## LENTIL SOUP WITH CHESTNUTS

Make the soup in the same way as the previous recipe, but substitute 8 oz (225 g) boiled chestnuts for the mussels. Boil the chestnuts in a separate pan and mash them before adding to the lentil soup. Add chopped parsley, chervil, tarragon and lovage.

# SPINACH SOUP

Several new vegetables became popular in the sixteenth century, including cauliflower, celery and asparagus. As a result the flavours of some traditional potherbs lost their appeal. Many of the flowers and leaves which had a place in the pottages of the Elizabethans, such as avens, mercury, primrose, violet and mallow, had been abandoned by the end of the eighteenth century. Green beets, mallows, orache, mercury, bugloss and others were all discarded in favour of spinach. Some herbs, however, were still in use then, though they are rarely used today: hyssop, chervil, purslane, and marigold flowers.

| | |
|---|---|
| 1 lb (450 g) spinach | 1 tablespoon chopped parsley |
| 1 small turnip | 1 teaspoon thyme |
| 1 onion | 2 pt (1·1 litres) stock |
| 2 carrots | freshly ground pepper |
| 2 sticks celery | salt |
| 2 tablespoons butter *or* cooking oil | |

Wash the spinach and shred it. Finely chop the rest of the vegetables. Heat the butter in a soup pan and add all the vegetables. Stir over a gentle heat for 5 minutes. Add the herbs and stock. Season with pepper and salt to taste and simmer for 20 minutes. Pass through a coarse sieve or put in a blender.

# TOMATO SOUP

| | |
|---|---|
| 1 tablespoon butter *or* cooking oil | 2–3 bay leaves |
| 1 onion, chopped | 2 pt (1·1 litres) stock |
| 2 medium carrots, grated | freshly ground pepper |
| 1 lb (450 g) tomatoes, chopped | salt |
| 2 cloves of garlic, finely chopped | 2 teaspoons finely chopped chives |
| ½ teaspoon thyme | single cream (optional) |
| ½ teaspoon marjoram *or* basil | |

Heat the butter in a soup pan and fry the onion over a gentle heat until transparent. Add the carrot and turn in the hot butter. Then add the tomatoes, garlic and herbs and turn them too in the butter. Pour the hot stock into the pan and season with pepper and salt to taste. Cover and simmer for 30 minutes. Pass through a sieve or put in a blender. Return to the pan and garnish with chopped chives. Serve with fried bread squares and, if desired, a teaspoon of single cream for each helping.

# WATERCRESS SOUP

8 oz (225 g) lean ham, diced | 2 blades mace
1 thick slice bread, crumbled | 2 bunches watercress
2 sticks celery, sliced | 2 pt (1·1 litres) stock
1 onion, chopped | freshly ground pepper
1 carrot, sliced | salt
4 cloves

Put the ham and the bread in a soup pan. Add the celery, onion, carrot, spices and watercress, reserving a few leaves for a garnish. Cover with half of the stock and bring to the boil. Simmer for 20 minutes. Add the rest of the stock and simmer for a further 20 minutes. Rub through a sieve or put in a blender. Season with pepper and salt to taste. Serve garnished with a little finely chopped watercress.

# Fish & Seafood

Fish are an excellent wholefood, any contamination being the result only of pollution in the sea. Lovers of fish are right to concern themselves about pollution levels, therefore, especially where shellfish in inland waters are concerned.

Fish should be bought fresh wherever possible. The eyes should be bright and not sunken, with the gills open and red. The skin should be moist and unbroken and the flesh firm. Frozen fish may often be of good quality, and experience will show you which are the best buys.

The fishmonger will clean the fish for you, though this is a simple operation which can also be done at home. Slit open the belly and scrape out the entrails carefully. Wash thoroughly with water. Roes should be well washed if they are to be used. Remove the head and tail unless the fish is to be served whole. Small fish which are served whole have their entrails removed by making a slit under the gills. Squeeze them out by pressing on the middle of the fish with the finger and thumb. If the fish are to be served with a sauce, they should be boned before adding the sauce.

Shellfish should only be bought in season, unless tinned. They are best bought alive. Oysters and mussels should be tightly closed when bought, and open after cooking. Throw away any that do not do this.

*See also the recipes for:*

Crab Soup
Eel Pie
Eel Soup
Fish Pie
Fish Sauce
Flounder Pie
Haddock Soup with Forcemeat Balls
Herring Pie
Lenten Fish Pie

Lentil Soup with Mussels
Mussel Soup
Newcastle Potted Salmon
Pike in Broth
Potted Shrimps
Potted Sprats
Potted Trout
Prawn Soup
White Fish Soup

## STEWED COCKLES

Cockles are in season all the year. In this recipe fish stock or broth may be substituted for the ale if preferred.

| | |
|---|---|
| 2 pt (1·1 litres) cockles | ½ teaspoon freshly ground pepper |
| 1 teaspoon rosemary | ½ pt (285 ml) ale *or* wine |
| 1 teaspoon rue *or* pennyroyal | chopped fresh parsley |

Wash the cockles well and put in a stew pan. Sprinkle with the herbs and pepper. Pour in the ale or wine and stew for 30 minutes, adding more liquid if necessary. Garnish with parsley and serve with toast.

## STEWED MUSSELS

Mussels are in season all the year. Scrub the shells well and wash in three waters. When you buy them, discard any that are open or which do not close when sharply tapped.

| | |
|---|---|
| 2 pt (1·1 litres) mussels | 1 tablespoon chopped parsley *or* |
| 2 tablespoons butter *or* cooking oil | coriander leaf |
| ½ onion, finely chopped | ½ pint (285 ml) wine |
| 2 spring onions, finely chopped | 1 tablespoon chopped chervil |
| ½ teaspoon freshly ground pepper | |

*for the optional sauce*

| | |
|---|---|
| ½ teaspoon celery seed | 2 teaspoons melted butter *or* |
| 1 teaspoon rue | cooking oil |
| 6 peppercorns | 1 teaspoon cornflour dissolved |
| ½ teaspoon salt | in ½ cup water |
| 1 teaspoon honey | |

Put the mussels in a pan and cover with water. Heat slowly until the mussels open (about 5 minutes). Remove the beards and any small weed-like growth. Leave the mussels on half the shell. In another pan, heat the butter and gently fry the onion until golden. Put in the spring onions and mussels and turn in the butter. Sprinkle over them the pepper and herbs and cover with the wine. Stew on a gentle heat for 5–10 minutes. Serve with a garnish of chopped fresh herbs such as chervil, or make a sauce.

For the sauce, pound the celery seed, rue, peppercorns and salt together. Stir in the honey and melted butter. Mix well and add the cornflour liquid. Drain the cooked mussels and add the liquid to the pounded mixture. Stir together well over a gentle heat, and pour it over the mussels.

## MUSSELS IN HERB SAUCE

| | |
|---|---|
| 2 pt (1·1 litres) shelled mussels | 1 small onion, chopped |
| 1 stick celery, sliced | ½ cup dry white wine |
| 1 bunch parsley, chopped | |

*for the sauce*

| | |
|---|---|
| ½ pint (285 ml) yogurt *or* cream | freshly ground pepper |
| 1 teaspoon mustard powder | 4 tablespoons chopped fresh herbs |
| juice of ½ lemon | |

Prepare the mussels as in the previous recipe and put in a pan with the celery, parsley and onion. Pour the wine into the pan and cook gently on a low heat for 5 minutes. In a bowl, add a small amount of yogurt to the mustard and stir together, making sure there are no lumps. Stir in the rest of the yogurt, then the lemon juice. Mix this well into the cooked mussels. Sprinkle with pepper and chopped herbs. Serve as a first course with fingers of toast.

# OYSTERS WITH LOVAGE SAUCE

English oysters are in season from September until the end of April.

| | |
|---|---|
| 24 oysters | 1 tablespoon chopped lovage |
| 1 pint (570 ml) wine | 1 tablespoon wine vinegar |
| ½ teaspoon freshly ground pepper | 1 teaspoon honey |

It is important to eat oysters fresh, when the shells are tightly closed. Allow 5 or 6 oysters per person. Wash the oysters in their shells. To open them, hold the thick part of the oyster in the palm of the hand and prise open with a strong, thin knife near the back. Then use the blade to cut the muscle which holds the two shells together. Put each oyster in a strainer over a bowl, so that any liquor may be saved for the sauce.

Put the oysters in a stew pan with the rest of the ingredients and any strained liquor. Cook together gently for 10 minutes.

# BUTTERED PRAWNS

Prawns and shrimps are available most of the year, and frozen ones can be bought all the year round.

| | |
|---|---|
| 2 tablespoons butter | freshly grated nutmeg |
| 1 cup dry white wine *or* sherry | 1 tablespoon chopped parsley |
| 1 lb (450 g) prawns *or* shrimps, cooked and shelled | |

*for the optional dressing*

| | |
|---|---|
| 2 cups dry white wine | 1 teaspoon rue |
| pinch of freshly ground pepper | 1 teaspoon honey |
| 1 teaspoon chopped lovage | 2 teaspoons wine vinegar |
| 1 teaspoon chopped mint | 1 tablespoon ground almonds |

Melt the butter in a frying pan over a gentle heat and add the wine. When the pan contents are warm add the prawns. Stir together for 5 minutes. Serve sprinkled with nutmeg and parsley. Alternatively dress the prawns in a sauce made by stirring together all the ingredients listed. Add the prawns and heat gently together for 5 minutes.

## SEAFOOD STEW

As with all stews, the ingredients listed below may be varied to suit your taste and what you have available. Try other herb combinations, such as marjoram and thyme.

| | |
|---|---|
| 1 cup mussels | 1 teaspoon rue |
| 6 oysters | ½ teaspoon freshly ground pepper |
| 2 tablespoons butter *or* cooking oil | 1 tablespoon chopped parsley *or* |
| 1 onion, chopped | coriander leaf |
| 1 cup shelled prawns | ½ pt (285 ml) white wine |
| 8 oz (225 g) fish pieces | ½ pt (285 ml) fish stock *or* water |
| 1 tablespoon ground almonds | salt |

First prepare the mussels and oysters as in the previous recipes. Heat the butter in a pan and gently fry the onion until transparent. Add the shellfish and fish and turn in the butter. Add the ground almonds, rue, pepper and parsley. Pour the wine and stock into the pan and cook together for 30 minutes. Add salt to taste and cook for a further 15 minutes.

## BAKED COD

In the seventeenth century the pastry 'coffin' was discontinued and fish came to be baked in an open dish, covered with a protective layer of breadcrumbs as in the dish that follows. Cod is in season all the year, but best between September and February.

| | |
|---|---|
| 2 lb (900 g) cod | 1 tablespoon chopped spring onion |
| 4 tablespoons melted butter *or* | 1 teaspoon sage |
| cooking oil | 1 teaspoon rosemary |
| juice of 1 lemon | 1 teaspoon thyme |
| 1 tablespoon chopped parsley | 2 tablespoons breadcrumbs |

Cut the cod in pieces, removing the large bones. Mix together a marinade consisting of half the melted butter, the lemon juice, parsley, spring onion and herbs. Put the cod in a baking dish and cover with the marinade. Leave for 30 minutes. Sprinkle with breadcrumbs and baste with the rest of the melted butter. Bake at gas mark 4, 350°F (180°C), for 30 minutes, or grill or fry using gentle heat. Serve with a suitable fish sauce (see Sauces chapter) if desired.

## STEWED COD

In the eighteenth century a few oysters, which were then cheap, would have been added with the lemon juice.

| | |
|---|---|
| 2 lb (900 g) cod | 1 small onion stuck with |
| freshly grated nutmeg |    4–6 cloves |
| freshly ground pepper | ½ pt (285 ml) white wine |
| 1 teaspoon salt | ¼ pt (140 ml) water |
| bunch of sweet herbs | juice of 1 lemon |

Cut the cod in pieces and season with nutmeg, pepper and salt. Put in a stew pan with the herbs and the clove onion. Pour in the wine and water. Put a lid on the pan and simmer for 5 minutes. Pour in the lemon juice. Cover again and stew until the fish is tender (20–30 minutes). Before serving, remove the onion and herbs.

## STEWED EELS

Eels are available all the year, especially between June and March. They need to be skinned before use. Hold the head with a cloth and cut through the skin at the neck. Pull the head with one hand and the skin with the other. The skin will tear off. Cut off the bristles which run up the back.

| | |
|---|---|
| 1 tablespoon butter *or* cooking oil | bunch of sweet herbs |
| 1 tablespoon flour | 3 cloves |
| 1 cup fish stock | 4 peppercorns |
| 1 pt (570 ml) white wine | 1 teaspoon salt |
| 2 tablespoons chopped onion | 2 lb (900 g) eels, cut in pieces |
| 2 tablespoons chopped mushrooms | 2–4 anchovies, chopped |
| 2 tablespoons chopped parsley | whole capers *or* nasturtium buds |

Heat the butter in a pan and stir in the flour. Add the stock and wine and stir together. Add the onion, mushrooms, parsley, herbs, spices and salt. Stew together until the onion is cooked. Put in the eels. Stew in the liquid until the fish is tender (35–45 minutes). Garnish with the anchovies and a few capers and serve with fried bread.

# HADDOCK WITH FORCEMEAT BALLS

Haddock is available all the year.

| | |
|---|---|
| 2 lb (900 g) haddock | 2 tablespoons finely chopped bacon |
| freshly ground pepper | 2 teaspoons finely chopped parsley |
| 2 tablespoons melted butter *or* | 1 teaspoon dried mixed herbs |
|    cooking oil | 1 tablespoon finely chopped onion |
| 2 tablespoons breadcrumbs | 1 egg, beaten |

Preheat the oven to gas mark 4, 350°F (180°C). Put the fish in a baking dish and sprinkle with pepper. Baste with the melted butter. Mix the rest of the ingredients together and squeeze into small balls. Arrange these around the pieces of fish. Cover with greaseproof paper and bake until the fish is cooked (30–40 minutes).

# HERRINGS WITH MUSTARD SAUCE

Herrings are in season from April to February, though their numbers are now scarce. It is well worth waiting for fresh specimens of this excellent fish. The use of mustard with herrings became popular in the eighteenth century. Here is a recipe with a simple sauce.

| | |
|---|---|
| 4–6 herrings | ½ pt (285 ml) milk |
| salt | 1 teaspoon mustard |
| freshly ground pepper | wine vinegar |
| butter *or* cooking oil for frying | 2 tablespoons chopped parsley |
| 1 tablespoon flour | |

Cut off the heads of the herrings, slit open and gut. Sprinkle with a little salt and pepper. Heat the butter and gently fry each herring for about 5 minutes. Keep warm. Make the sauce by putting the melted butter from the fried herrings into a saucepan. Add the flour and stir for 1 minute. Gradually add the milk and keep stirring until the sauce thickens. Mix the mustard powder with sufficient wine vinegar to make a thin cream. Stir into the sauce. Serve the herrings accompanied by the sauce and garnished with chopped parsley.

# BAKED MACKEREL

Mackerel are available all the year, especially from February to October. They should always be eaten very fresh.

| | |
|---|---|
| 4–6 mackerel | 4–6 cloves, ground |
| sea salt | bay leaves |
| powdered mace | wine vinegar |
| freshly ground pepper | melted butter |

Preheat the oven to gas mark 4, 350°F (180°C). Cut off the heads of the fish, slit open and gut. Rub with a little salt. Sprinkle with mace, pepper and cloves. Place in the bottom of a baking dish a piece of foil large enough to fold over and form a parcel. Lay in the fish. Put on a few bay leaves, a sprinkling of wine vinegar and a little melted butter. Wrap the foil tightly over the fish and bake for 15–20 minutes.

# STEWED MACKEREL

| | |
|---|---|
| 4–6 mackerel | 1 onion, finely chopped |
| salt | freshly ground pepper |
| ½ pt (285 ml) white wine | 2 tablespoons lemon juice |
| ½ pt (285 ml) stock | 2 tablespoons finely |
| bunch of sweet herbs | chopped fennel *or* parsley |
| 1 carrot, grated | |

Cut off the heads of the fish, slit open and gut. Rub with a little salt. Make a sauce by boiling gently together the wine, stock, herbs, carrot and onion. After 10 minutes add salt and pepper to taste. Boil for another 15 minutes. Lay the fish in a stewing dish and pour the sauce over it. Stew gently until the fish is tender (10–15 minutes). Serve sprinkled with lemon juice and chopped herbs.

## STEWED MULLET

Mullet is in season all the year. Red mullet is the most suitable kind for this recipe.

| | |
|---|---|
| 4 mullet | 2 tablespoons finely |
| sea salt | chopped onion |
| juice of 1 lemon | bunch of sweet herbs |
| freshly ground pepper | freshly grated nutmeg |
| 2 glasses red wine | 2–4 anchovies |

Simmer the mullet in a little salted water for 10 minutes. Add the lemon juice, pepper, wine, onion, herbs, nutmeg and anchovy. Simmer together for 15 minutes and serve the fish with some of the sauce poured over.

## MARINATED PIKE

Pikes are in season from 1 June until 15 March. This recipe is from the eighteenth century. Use the quantities listed below for each pike you serve. Herbs that go well with this fish are thyme, savory, marjoram and chives.

| | |
|---|---|
| salt | 2 tablespoons chopped onion |
| 1 cup wine | 2 bay leaves |
| 2 tablespoons wine vinegar | 2 peppercorns |
| 1 pt (570 ml) water | 4 cloves |
| small bunch of sweet herbs | 2 teaspoons cornflour |
| a few small pieces of | a few sliced mushrooms |
| lemon peel | lemon juice |

Clean the pike, cut into steaks and lay in a dish. Sprinkle with a little salt. Boil the wine and wine vinegar together. Remove from the heat and allow to cool for 2 minutes. Pour the liquid over the pike and allow to marinate for 2 hours. Put the water in a pan with the herbs, lemon peel, onion, bay leaves, peppercorns and cloves. Boil for 15 minutes, then add the marinated pike and stew over a gentle heat until tender (5–10 minutes).

To make a sauce, remove the fish and keep the liquid. In a saucepan stir a cupful of the cooled liquid gradually into the cornflour, making sure there are no lumps. Add to the rest of the liquid. Put in the mushrooms and keep the sauce on a low heat until it thickens. Add lemon juice to taste, and serve with the pike.

# FRIED PLAICE WITH HERB SAUCE

Prepare 2–3 fish as follows:

| | |
|---|---|
| 2 eggs, beaten | freshly ground pepper |
| breadcrumbs, lightly browned | salt |
| butter and olive oil for frying | 2 cloves |
| 1 anchovy | 1 blade of mace |
| 1 teaspoon thyme | 2 teaspoons flour |
| 1 tablespoon chopped parsley | 1–2 tablespoons lemon juice |

Cut the fins off closely and cut round the head and tail. Cut through the flesh down to the bone which marks the middle of the fish. Slip the blade of the knife along the bone under the flesh until the fillets come off whole from each side of the spine. Turn the fish over and remove the other two fillets. Make sure that the fillets are dry. Pour the beaten egg into a dish. Put the breadcrumbs on a sheet of paper. Lay each fillet first in the egg, and brush well, then into the crumbs, and shake the crumbs over both sides. Put the fillets on one side to harden for a while.

Butter has a good flavour but burns quickly, whereas olive oil will not burn until it reaches around double that temperature. A mixture of the two will retain the flavour but prevent the butter from burning too quickly during the frying. Heat the mixture and fry the fish gently until cooked, then put them on a dish and keep warm. Keep the butter and oil mixture in the pan.

Make the sauce by boiling the bones in a little water for 10 minutes. Add the anchovy, thyme, parsley, pepper and salt to taste, cloves and mace. Simmer gently until the anchovy breaks down. Gently heat the butter and oil mixture that the fish was fried in and add the flour. Stir until it browns. Add the strained fishbone liquor and let it boil until it thickens. Add the lemon juice. Serve the fish pieces with the sauce poured over them.

# BAKED SALMON

Salmon is available all the year, but English salmon is best from February to September. Here is another two-hundred-year-old recipe.

| | |
|---|---|
| 2 lb (900 g) salmon pieces | 2–4 mushrooms, sliced |
| 2 tablespoons melted butter *or* cooking oil | freshly ground pepper |
| | salt |
| 2 tablespoons chopped parsley | breadcrumbs |
| 1–2 spring onions, chopped | melted butter *or* cooking oil |
| small bunch of sweet herbs | for basting |

Preheat the oven to gas mark 4, 350°F (180°C). Wash the salmon pieces and allow to drain. Mix the butter in a bowl with the parsley, spring onion, herbs, mushrooms, pepper and salt to taste. Put half of this mixture in the bottom of a baking dish. Lay thin slices of salmon on top. Cover with the rest of the mixture. Strew some breadcrumbs over the top and baste with a little melted butter. Bake in a moderate oven until cooked (10 minutes). Serve with a relish or sauce.

## STUFFED SALMON TROUT

In his *English Art of Cookery*, Richard Briggs considered this eighteenth-century recipe 'a very elegant dish for a genteel company'. As a final touch, he would have garnished it with fish patties and barberries. Salmon trout is in season from March until August.

| | |
|---|---|
| 1 large salmon trout | 1 egg, beaten |
| 1 eel | fish stock |
| 2 anchovies | white wine |
| 1–2 teaspoons grated lemon peel | 2 tablespoons chopped herbs |
| grated nutmeg | 2 tablespoons chopped onion *or* |
| 1 tablespoon chopped parsley | chives |
| 1–2 teaspoons chopped thyme | 1 teaspoon powdered mace |
| 1 tablespoon breadcrumbs | 2 tablespoons butter *or* |
| freshly ground pepper | cooking oil |
| salt | 1 tablespoon flour |

Clean and wash the salmon trout and eel. Cut the eel flesh from the bones and chop. Put in a bowl. Add the anchovies, grated lemon peel, grated nutmeg, parsley, thyme, breadcrumbs, and pepper and salt to taste. Stir in the egg. Put this mixture in the belly of the salmon trout and sew up using ordinary needle and thread. Lay the fish in a fish kettle or pan just big enough to hold it. Just cover it with a mixture of stock and wine. Sprinkle on top the herbs, onion and mace and stew the fish gently (20–30 minutes) until tender. Strain off the juice.

In a saucepan melt the butter and stir in the flour. Allow to brown gently. Add the fish juice and stir together until well blended. Cut and remove the thread and serve the fish with the sauce poured over it.

# STEWED SKATE

Skate is in season from October until May.

| | |
|---|---|
| 2–3 lb (900 g–1·3 kg) skate | ½ teaspoon salt |
| 1 pt (570 ml) stock *or* water | ¼ pt (140 ml) cream *or* yogurt |
| 1 teaspoon powdered mace | small knob of butter rolled in flour |
| grated nutmeg | 1 glass white wine |
| small bunch of sweet herbs | lemon slices |

Cut the skate flesh from the bones in slices. Lay in a saucepan. Pour in the stock. Add the mace, grated nutmeg to taste, herbs and salt. Cover and simmer gently for 15 minutes. Add the cream, butter and wine. Shake the pan to prevent sticking, and cook until the sauce is thick and smooth. Serve garnished with lemon.

# BRAISED SOLE

Sole is obtainable all the year, but is considered off season in April and May.

| | |
|---|---|
| 2–3 lb (900 g–1·3 kg) sole | grated nutmeg |
| flour | 1 teaspoon finely chopped fresh |
| cooking oil for frying | ginger |
| claret *or* white wine *or* dry cider | lemon slices |
| 1–2 anchovies, chopped | |

Clean and skin the fish. Remove the fins, then make a cut across the root of the tail. Slip your thumb under the skin. Grip the tail firmly and pull the flap of skin towards the head. Dry the fish and roll it in flour. Heat enough oil in a frying pan to fry the sole gently on both sides until just golden. Then put the fish in a saucepan and pour over it just enough wine to cover. Add the anchovy, nutmeg to taste and ginger. Stew gently until half the liquor is used up. Serve garnished with lemon slices.

# STEWED SOLE

This recipe is also good for turbot, plaice, flounders or dabs.

| | |
|---|---|
| 2–3 lb (900 g–1·3 kg) sole | 2 tablespoons butter *or* |
| 2 teaspoons basil | cooking oil |
| 2 teaspoons thyme | 1 tablespoon flour |
| 2 teaspoons marjoram | 1–2 anchovies, chopped |
| 2 tablespoons chopped parsley | 1–2 tablespoons capers *or* |
| 2 tablespoons chopped chives | nasturtium buds |
| 2 tablespoons chopped onions | freshly ground pepper |
| white wine | salt |
| white wine vinegar | grated nutmeg |

Wash and dry the fish. In a bowl mix the herbs and onion together. Strew half the mixture in the bottom of a stew pan. Lay in the fish. Strew over it the rest of the herb mixture. Pour in equal quantities of wine and vinegar until the fish is covered. Stew on a gentle heat until the fish is tender (9–10 minutes). Remove from the heat.

In a saucepan heat the butter and stir in the flour. Add 1 tablespoon of vinegar, 1 cup of water, the anchovies, capers, pepper, salt and nutmeg to taste. Remove the fish from the pan. Pour the liquor into the saucepan and heat up the sauce gently until it thickens. Serve the fish with the sauce poured over it.

# BAKED TROUT

Wild trout are in season from February to September, but farm trout are now available at reasonable cost at most times of the year. Allow one small trout per person. Use the following ingredients for each trout.

| | |
|---|---|
| 1–2 tablespoons chopped *or* | grated nutmeg |
| ground almonds | 1 egg, beaten |
| 1–2 tablespoons breadcrumbs | melted butter *or* cooking oil |
| pinch of salt | red wine |
| freshly ground pepper | lemon juice |
| 2–4 cloves, ground | |

Trout are served with their heads intact. If you intend baking the fish, preheat the oven to gas mark 4, 350°F (180°C). Wash the trout, remove the gills and allow the fish to dry. In a bowl, mix together the almonds, breadcrumbs, salt, pepper, cloves, nutmeg and egg. Put the fish on a baking tray and spread the mixture over it. Baste with butter and wine. Bake for 10 minutes or grill gently until tender. Serve sprinkled with a little lemon juice.

## BARBECUED FISH

This is a recipe modified from the traditional method of roasting fish on a spit.

Clean the fish and wash them. Place them, open, on the barbecue. Sprinkle with chopped herbs, salt and pepper, and baste with melted butter. When the fish are cooked, serve garnished with slices of lemon or orange. Other excellent garnishes are gooseberries, grapes, redcurrants, chopped parsley or fennel.

## FISH STEW

When the Romans brought Mediterranean herbs to Britain, these made the peasant fish stew much tastier. Fish consumption declined once the Romans had left and only increased when the Church introduced religious fasting days on which only fish-eating was permitted. In the Middle Ages cereals were added to fish stews along with spices to make rich, thick pottages.

| | |
|---|---|
| 2 lb (900 g) fish | 1 pint stock |
| 2 tablespoons melted butter | 1 teaspoon salt |
| 2 tablespoons olive oil | freshly ground pepper |
| 1 lb (450 g) leeks, chopped | 2 teaspoons lovage |
| 2 tablespoons chopped parsley *or* coriander leaf | 1 teaspoon marjoram |
| | 1 teaspoon basil |
| 1 cup wine | |

Clean and wash the fish and cut in pieces. Heat the butter and oil in a stew pan and turn the fish until all the pieces are well covered. Add the leeks, parsley and the rest of the ingredients. Stew together gently for 30 minutes, adding more liquid if necessary. To make a more substantial meal, serve with bread or some other vegetables.

# BAKED OR GRILLED FISH
# WITH MUSTARD SAUCE

4–6 fish fillets
2–4 anchovies, chopped
2–4 cloves garlic, finely chopped
1–2 teaspoons mustard powder

1 tablespoon melted butter
lemon juice
lemon slices

If you intend baking the fish, preheat the oven to gas mark 4, 350°F (180°C). Arrange the fish on a baking dish. In a bowl mix together the anchovies, garlic, mustard and butter. Moisten with lemon juice to make a paste, and spread it over the fish. Bake or grill for 15–20 minutes until the fish is cooked. Serve with lemon slices.

# FISH STOCK

Any fish may be used in this recipe, along with fish trimmings, but avoid oily fish such as mackerel, salmon or herring. Dark pieces of skin also discolour the stock. This recipe, which dates from the mid-nineteenth century, can be used as a base for soups or sauces or for stewing other fish. Other vegetables of your choice may be added, but take care not to overpower the flavour of the fish.

1 lb (450 g) fish
1½ pt (855 ml) water
chopped celery
chopped parsley
chopped onion

bunch of sweet herbs
powdered mace
freshly ground pepper
salt

Cut the fish into pieces. Put it in a large stew pan and cover with the water. Add the chopped celery, parsley and onion and the bunch of sweet herbs. Season with powdered mace, freshly ground pepper and salt to taste. Simmer gently for 30 minutes, adding more water if necessary. Strain. Reduce the stock to a small, concentrated quantity, and freeze in cubes in an ice tray.

# Meat & Offal

All English meat, whether it is of ox, calf, sheep, or swine has a fatness and a delicious taste, either because of the excellent pasture, which consists of such nourishing and sweet-scented kinds of hay as there are in this country, or some way of fattening the cattle known to the butchers alone.

Per Kalm – *Account of his Visit to England*, 1748

*See also the recipes for:*

| | |
|---|---|
| Creamed Pork Pottage | Pork Pie |
| Kidney Pie | Potted Beef |
| Lamb Pie | Sausage and Prune Stuffing |
| Marble Veal | Spicy Mutton Pie |
| Meat Pottage | Steak and Kidney Pie |
| Medley Pie | Sweet Lamb Pie |
| Pork and Herb Paste | Veal Pie |

# GRILLED VEAL

In the eighteenth century, a more exotic version of this dish was created by making slits in thick slices of veal and stuffing them with washed oysters. Slices of lemon accompanied the veal.

| | |
|---|---|
| 1½ lb (680 g) veal, cut in pieces | freshly ground pepper |
| breadcrumbs | grated nutmeg *or* powdered |
| finely chopped parsley | cinnamon |
| thyme | salt |
| marjoram | 2 eggs, beaten |

Beat the veal slices well with a wooden beater or rolling pin. Mix the breadcrumbs with the herbs, spices and salt to taste. Brush the veal slices with egg on both sides and dip them in the seasoned breadcrumbs. Grill under a medium heat for 7–10 minutes, turning frequently, or broil in a lightly greased hot pan. Serve with mushrooms, meat balls (see recipe for Meat Balls) and sprigs of watercress.

# ROAST MARINATED VEAL

Whitsun was a season for walks and village feasts. Joints of cold beef, legs of mutton, ham, meat pies, pressed beef, pickled onions and salads, jellies, custards, fruit tarts and cheese – such would be the dinner served on the village green. Traditional Whitsun food in Sussex was roast veal and gooseberry pudding.

This rich way of cooking veal below was adapted by Mrs Cole (see Bibliography). Choose a joint of fillet, loin or best end of neck. The meat must be marinated the day before roasting.

3–4 lb (1·3–1·8 kg) joint of veal

*for the marinade*

| | |
|---|---|
| 2 pt (1·1 litres) milk | 3 bay leaves |
| 1 lemon, peeled and sliced | 2 teaspoons thyme |
| 2 cloves of garlic, chopped | 1 tablespoon chopped parsley |
| 1 onion, chopped | 4–6 peppercorns |
| 4 cloves | 1 teaspoon salt |

*for cooking the veal*

butter | bacon rashers

*for the sauce*

cream | 1 teaspoon cornflour

Wash the joint and dry it. Make the marinade by mixing the milk in a bowl with the rest of the marinade ingredients. Warm the marinade. Put the veal in a pot just big enough to hold it and pour the marinade over it. Allow to marinate for 12 hours.

Next day, preheat the oven to gas mark 6, 400°F (200°C). Remove the veal from the marinade and smear it with a little butter. Put it in a baking tin and lay some pieces of bacon on top. Roast for 15 minutes, then reduce the heat to gas mark 2, 300°F (150°C). Baste the joint from time to time. Allow about 25 minutes total cooking time per 1 lb (450 g) weight.

A cream sauce can be made by gently heating a pint of the marinade and adding cream until the required consistency is reached. Thicken by first adding a teaspoon of cornflour to a cup of marinade and then stirring this mixture into the sauce.

# ROAST BEEF, TUDOR STYLE

In the twelfth and thirteenth centuries beef emerged as the favourite flesh meat of the English and it has remained so.

Buy your meat on the bone and cook it that way. Like a skewer in a baked potato, the bone conducts the heat to the inside of the joint and holds the meat together. Choose a double rib joint or, if you want something special, a good piece of sirloin. Leftover beef can always be eaten with a relish or pickles the next day. It is delicious with a salad and jacket potatoes or in a sandwich.

In former times, roasting meant exposing meat to the heat of an open fire. To make sure that it was cooked evenly the meat was fixed to a wooden or metal spit which could be revolved over the fire. Today the grill or barbecue is the nearest equivalent to true roasting. The modern oven efficiently conserves heat so that the meat is baked as well as roasted.

Preheat the oven to gas mark 6, 400°F (200°C). Moisten the base of a roasting tin with melted butter, beef dripping or cooking oil, and put in the joint. Prepare the joint for roasting by sprinkling with a mixture of ground cinnamon, cloves, mace and freshly ground pepper. Dredge with fine breadcrumbs, flour or oatmeal. Finally baste with a little melted butter, beef dripping or cooking oil. The dredging layer protects the surface of the meat from drying as it cooks. Do not add salt since this encourages meat juices to escape from the joint.

Cook the joint for 15 minutes, then reduce the heat to gas mark 2, 200°F (150°C). Allow about 15–25 minutes cooking time per 1 lb (450 g) weight, according to whether you want the meat rare or well done.

Serve with Yorkshire pudding and horseradish sauce.

# COLLARED BEEF

In the seventeenth century, the English seem to have produced more cookery books than even the Italians or the French. This recipe is adapted from *The Queens Closet Opened* of 1688, which was compiled by 'the most Experienced Persons of the Times'.

| | |
|---|---|
| 3 lb (1·3 kg) brisket *or* topside *or* silverside | 1 teaspoon thyme |
| | 1 teaspoon chopped sage |
| salt | broken bay leaf |
| freshly ground pepper | 1–2 cloves of garlic, |
| 2 allspice berries, ground | finely chopped |

Trim the meat and beat it flat. Sprinkle with the seasoning, herbs and spices. Roll it up tightly and tie with string at each end and at the middle. Put it in a stew pot and cover with cold water. Bring to the boil, removing any scum. Allow to simmer gently for 3 hours. Serve hot or cold with vegetables and horseradish sauce.

# BRAISED BEEF

By the fifteenth century, braising had been developed to make what was known as a dry stew. Originally the ingredients were enclosed in a vessel which was suspended inside a cauldron of gently boiling water. This method of braising still lives on today as jugged steak, in which the ingredients are packed in a stoneware jar which is sealed, placed in a pan of boiling water, and allowed to simmer on the top of the stove or in the oven for 2 hours. No extra water or fat is added. For a true fifteenth-century taste, add cloves, mace and currants to the beef. This is a more modern recipe for braised beef.

| | |
|---|---|
| 3 tablespoons melted butter *or* cooking oil | 1 teaspoon thyme |
| | a few bay leaves |
| 6 oz (170 g) bacon, cut in small pieces | 1 tablespoon chopped parsley |
| | 2 strips lemon peel |
| 1 onion, chopped | 2–4 cloves of garlic, finely chopped |
| 3 lb (1·3 kg) braising beef, cut in small cubes | ale *or* wine |
| | freshly ground pepper |
| 2–3 carrots, sliced | chopped fresh herbs to garnish |

Preheat the oven to gas mark 2, 300°F (150°C). Heat the butter in a pan and gently fry the bacon and onion until the onion is transparent. Add the beef and fry until it begins to brown. Add the carrots and stir until they are well covered with butter. Add the herbs and garlic. Pour over enough ale or wine to cover. Add stock if necessary. Season with pepper to taste. Bring to the boil, turn down the heat and cover. Put in the oven for 2–3 hours. Serve garnished with fresh herbs.

## SUSSEX HOTPOT

| | |
|---|---|
| 8 oz–1 lb (225–450 g) small onions *or* shallots, chopped | peppercorns a few bay leaves |
| 2–4 sticks celery, chopped | wine vinegar |
| 2 lb (900 g) best stewing beef, cut in cubes | 2 lb (900 g) potatoes, cut in thick slices |
| allspice | stock |
| cloves | |

Preheat the oven to gas mark 3, 325°F (170°C). Put half the onions and celery in a large casserole dish. Add half the beef. Sprinkle with a few whole allspice, cloves, peppercorns, bay leaves and a tablespoon of vinegar. Cover with a layer of sliced potato. Add a second layer of beef and spices. Top with the rest of the onion and celery and a second layer of potato slices. Pour stock into the dish until it nearly covers the potatoes. Cover, and cook in the oven for 2 hours. Remove the lid and cook for a further hour. If the potatoes are not browning enough, turn up the heat for the last 15 minutes.

## BEEF STEW WITH DUMPLINGS

Seventeenth-century writers noted that poorer people were still making do with tougher pieces of meat which were unsuitable for roasting. This meat was first beaten or chopped up and fried, which would seal the surfaces and lock in the juices, then stewed with herbs or onions and spices until tender. Things do not seem to have changed much three centuries later. In this recipe, tasty dumplings are used to fill out the dish.

| | |
|---|---|
| salt | 2 lb (900 g) stewing steak, cut in cubes |
| freshly ground pepper | |
| ground mace | 4 medium onions, sliced |
| 3 oz (85 g) flour | 4 medium carrots, sliced |
| 4–6 tablespoons beef dripping *or* cooking oil | 2 pt (1·1 litres) stock |

*for the dumplings*

| | |
|---|---|
| 3 oz (85 g) flour | 2 teaspoons dried mixed herbs *or* |
| ¼ teaspoon baking powder | ½ teaspoon each of rosemary, |
| 1 teaspoon salt | sage, thyme and marjoram |
| ½ teaspoon freshly ground pepper | 1 oz (30 g) shredded suet |
| | a little milk |

Sift ½ teaspoon each of salt, pepper and mace into the flour. Roll the beef pieces in the flour to coat them. Heat the fat in a large pan and gently brown the meat. Remove from the pan. Add the onion and carrots and fry them in the remaining fat until the onion softens. Stir in any remaining seasoned flour. Gradually add the stock and bring to the boil. Lower the heat and return the meat to the pan. Add more seasoning if required. Allow to simmer for 1½ hours.

Meanwhile make the dumplings. Sift the flour into a bowl with the baking powder, salt and pepper. Stir in the herbs and suet. Add enough milk to make a stiff dough. Divide into 8 portions and shape into balls. Place in the stew and allow to simmer for a further 30 minutes.

## STEWED STEAK

Apart from Christmas, the most important meal of the rural year was the harvest-home or mell-supper. This was one of the few occasions when a farm labourer might have beef. Preparations for such feasts in the barn or farm kitchen went on all day. On prosperous farms, chicken, hare, beef, bacon and ham were eaten along with cheese, tarts, custards, ginger cake and plum puddings. These would be washed down with home-made wine, beer and cider.

> Here's health unto our master,
> The founder of the feast!

Here is an eighteenth-century beef stew which has been adapted from one designed for a large gathering on a festive occasion.

| | |
|---|---|
| 1½ lb (680 g) stewing steak | 1 teaspoon powdered mace |
| salt | 4 cloves |
| freshly ground pepper | 2 teaspoons sweet herbs |
| 2 oz (60 g) flour | 1 cup red wine |
| 2 tablespoons beef dripping | 1 cup stock |
| *or* butter *or* cooking oil | 1–2 anchovies, chopped |
| 1 onion, chopped | |

Cut the steak into small pieces. Sprinkle with salt and pepper and roll in flour. Heat the fat in a large pan and fry the onion until transparent. Add the steak, mace, cloves and herbs and continue frying until the steak begins to brown. Add the wine, stock and anchovy. Cover and stew gently for about 1 hour, or until the steak is tender.

## STEWED STEAK WITH MUSHROOM AND WINE SAUCE

| | |
|---|---|
| 8 oz (225 g) bacon *or* ham | grated nutmeg |
| 8 oz (225 g) mushrooms, chopped | ½ pt (285 ml) yogurt *or* cream |
| 1 small onion, chopped | 1½ lb (680 g) stewing steak, cut in |
| 2 tablespoons chopped parsley | pieces |
| 2 teaspoons thyme | 2 tablespoons butter *or* cooking oil |
| 2 teaspoons grated lemon peel | 1 pint (570 ml) stock |
| yolks of 4 eggs | 1 cup red wine |

Chop the bacon finely. Put it in a bowl and mix with the mushrooms, onion, parsley, thyme, lemon peel, eggs, nutmeg and yogurt. Beat the steak and fry it in butter for 5 minutes in a deep pan. Add the chopped bacon mixture and fry together for 5 minutes. Add the stock and wine and simmer for about 1½ hours until the meat is tender.

## MARINATED LAMB

Scrag end of neck is ideal for this dish, but chops or pieces of fillet would do equally well.

2 lb (900 g) lamb
1 pt (570 ml) stock
1 cup wine

*for the marinade*

| | |
|---|---|
| 2 tablespoons wine vinegar | 2 cloves of garlic, finely |
| 2 peppercorns, ground | chopped |
| ½ teaspoon salt | 1 small onion, sliced |
| 4 cloves, ground | 2 teaspoons thyme |

butter *or* cooking oil for frying

Cut the lamb into pieces and gently stew them in the stock and wine until nearly tender. Meanwhile mix up the marinade ingredients in a bowl. Add a cup of the stewing stock and then the lamb pieces. Mix well and allow to marinate for 1 hour. Remove from the marinade and fry until golden. Make a gravy from any leftover stewing stock and marinade mixture.

## STEWED LAMB CHOPS

| | |
|---|---|
| 4 cloves | 1 onion, chopped |
| 2 peppercorns | a few pieces of rosemary |
| freshly grated nutmeg | salt |
| ½ teaspoon powdered mace | butter |
| 4 lamb chops | flour |
| ½ pt (285 ml) stock | slices of lemon |
| 1 cup white wine | |

Grind together the cloves and peppercorns. Add the nutmeg and mace. Season the chops with this mixture. Lay them in a stew pan and add the stock, wine, onion and rosemary. Sprinkle with a little salt and stew gently until the chops are tender. Thicken the gravy with a small piece of butter rolled in flour. Serve the chops with the gravy and lemon slices.

## FRIED LAMB CHOPS

| | |
|---|---|
| 1 egg, beaten | 2 teaspoons savory |
| ½ cup breadcrumbs | 2 teaspoons grated lemon peel |
| 2 tablespoons chopped parsley | 4 lamb chops |
| 2 teaspoons thyme | butter *or* cooking oil for frying |
| 2 teaspoons marjoram *or* rosemary | slices of lemon |

In a bowl mix the egg, breadcrumbs, parsley, herbs and lemon peel. Rub the chops on both sides with this mixture. Fry in butter until lightly golden. Serve garnished with the lemon slices.

## LAMB CUTLET FRICASSEE

Use leg of lamb cut across the grain.

| | |
|---|---|
| 2 lb (900 g) lamb cutlets | ¼ teaspoon chilli powder |
| butter *or* cooking oil for frying | 1 cup sliced mushrooms |
| 1 pt (570 ml) stock | 3 egg yolks, beaten with ½ pt |
| small bunch of sweet herbs | (285 ml) cream *or* yogurt |
| 1 onion, chopped | grated nutmeg |
| 2–4 cloves | sliced cooked beetroot |
| ½ teaspoon powdered mace | sliced lemon |
| ½ teaspoon salt | |

Fry the cutlets gently in butter for 5 minutes on both sides. Put them in a stew pan and cover with the stock, herbs, onion, cloves and mace; stew gently for 10 minutes. Remove the cutlets and keep them warm. Season the stock with a little salt and chilli powder. Add the mushrooms and egg yolk mixture. Stir together and add the cutlets. Sprinkle with freshly grated nutmeg and thoroughly reheat the dish. Serve garnished with beetroot and lemon slices.

## ROAST LAMB

There are many joints of lamb which are ideal for roasting, including hind- and fore-quarter, leg, shoulder, loin and breast. Shoulder is considered by some to have the sweetest meat because of the layers of fat which keep the meat moist during roasting. Roasting methods are traditional and have hardly changed. Henry Buttes, writing in *Dyets Dry Dinner*, published in 1599, suggested a recipe on these lines.

Preheat the oven to gas mark 6, 400°F (200°C). Rub every part of the joint with the cut end of a garlic clove. Sprinkle with pepper. Place in a roasting pan on a bed of sliced onion. Sprinkle well with sprigs of sage and rosemary. You may like to push pieces of garlic into the joint, and you use more than one clove for this purpose since it gives an excellent flavour to lamb.

Cook the joint for 15 minutes, then reduce the heat to gas mark 2, 300°F (150°C), and baste occasionally. Allow 20–25 minutes cooking time per 1 lb (450 g) weight.

There is really nothing better than mint sauce as an accompaniment to roast lamb.

## LAMB STEW

| | |
|---|---|
| 2 lb (900 g) lamb (scrag end of neck) | 1 teaspoon salt |
| | sprig of lovage |
| 2 tablespoons butter *or* cooking oil | sprig of thyme |
| | 1 teaspoon cumin powder |
| 1 onion, chopped | 1 pt (570 ml) stock |
| freshly ground pepper | 1 glass wine |

Cut the lamb into pieces. Heat the butter in a stew pan and fry the onion until transparent. Add the lamb pieces. Fry gently for 5 minutes. Sprinkle with pepper, salt, lovage, thyme and cumin. Pour the stock and wine into the pan and stew gently for about 1½ hours until the meat is tender.

Vegetables such as potatoes, carrots and mushrooms may be added to this stew.

# MUTTON CUTLETS, LOVER'S FASHION

This recipe is from an eighteenth-century cookery book, but the writer does not say what makes this method 'lover's fashion'. My guess is that lovers always appreciate tasty food.

| | |
|---|---|
| 2 lb (900 g) best mutton cutlets | 1 onion, sliced |
| butter *or* cooking oil | 2 carrots, sliced |
| finely chopped parsley | 1 parsnip, sliced |
| chopped savory | 4 oz (110 g) chopped ham *or* bacon |
| freshly ground pepper | 1 cup white wine |
| salt | 1 pt (570 ml) stock |

Smear the cutlets with butter. Sprinkle with parsley, savory, pepper and salt. Fry the onion, carrots and parsnip in a little butter in a stew pan for 5 minutes. Add the cutlets and fry for a further 5 minutes. Add the ham, wine and stock, and stew for about 1½ hours or until the meat and vegetables are tender.

# ROAST MUTTON

In the 1750s Anne Battam published *The Lady's Assistant in the Oeconomy of the Table*, which was considered by her London publishers as a collection of scarce and valuable receipts. Her roasting recipes all use ample quantities of herbs. Oysters were cheap and plentiful then – unlike today. For a special occasion, a shoulder of mutton stuffed in this way will give you the authentic taste of two centuries ago.

| | |
|---|---|
| 1 shoulder of mutton | 1 cup breadcrumbs |
| 12–24 oysters | 2 egg yolks |
| thyme | freshly grated nutmeg |
| parsley | freshly ground pepper |
| marjoram | salt |

*for the gravy*

| | |
|---|---|
| 1 cup white wine | freshly grated nutmeg |
| 1 small onion, sliced | small piece of butter |
| 2 cloves | flour |

Wash and dry the mutton joint. Preheat the oven to gas mark 6, 400°F (200°C). Clean the oysters and open them (instructions are given in the recipe for Oysters in Lovage Sauce). Wash them from their shells into a saucepan along with the liquor. Add a cup of water and stew the oysters gently for 5 minutes. Take a good quantity of herbs, chop finely and put in a bowl. Add the breadcrumbs, egg yolks, nutmeg, pepper and salt. Roll half the oysters in this mixture. Cut slits in the thick part of the mutton and stuff with the oysters and the herb mixture. Put the joint in a roasting pan and roast for 15 minutes. Reduce the heat to gas mark 2, 300°F (150°C), and roast the joint for 25 minutes per 1 lb (450 g) weight. Baste occasionally.

Halfway through the cooking take a little of the juice in the bottom of the pan to make gravy. Put the wine, onion, cloves, nutmeg and the rest of the oysters into a small pan. Stew together for 5 minutes and then stir into the pan the juice from the roasting pan. Serve the cooked mutton with the gravy, which may be thickened by adding a small piece of butter rolled in flour.

# LANCASHIRE HOTPOT

Some cooks like to stew the meat in a covered stockpot without browning first; this recipe, however, uses the browning method. Choose best end of neck of mutton or lamb. A variation of this recipe is Cumberland Hotpot, in which beef and slices of black pudding are substituted for lamb. Earlier hot pots also contained mushrooms and oysters.

| | |
|---|---|
| 2 lb (900 g) best end of neck | chopped herbs |
| 4 sheep's kidneys | freshly ground pepper |
| dripping *or* butter *or* cooking oil for frying | salt |
| | 2 teaspoons flour |
| 2 onions, chopped | 1 pt (570 ml) stock |
| 2 lb (900 g) potatoes, cut in thick slices | |

Preheat the oven to gas mark 3, 325°F (170°C). Trim the lamb and cut it into pieces. Skin, core and chop the kidneys. Heat the fat in a pan and fry the onions until transparent. Add the meat pieces and brown gently. Make a layer of the meat in the bottom of an ovenproof dish (traditionally this was a deep brown earthenware pot). Brown the kidneys in the fat left in the pan. Cover the lamb with layers of kidney, onion and potato. Season each layer with herbs, pepper and salt. The final layer should be of potato slices. Stir the flour into a cup of stock and add to the rest of the stock. Pour the stock over the meat and potato layers until it reaches the top layer. Cover closely and cook in the oven for 2 hours. Remove the lid and cook for a further 30 minutes to brown the top layer of potatoes. Serve with red cabbage.

## PORK WITH LEEKS

The Romans were very fond of leeks and by the Middle Ages leeks had become particularly popular among the Celts and the people of the North Country.

| | |
|---|---|
| dripping *or* butter *or* cooking oil for frying | 1 lb (450 g) cooking apples, peeled, cored and sliced |
| 2 lb (900 g) pork loin chops, cut in pieces | 4–6 peppercorns |
| 1 pt (570 ml) stock | 1 teaspoon coriander seeds |
| 1 lb (450 g) leeks, chopped | 1 tablespoon mint leaves |
| 2 tablespoons chopped parsley | wine vinegar |
| 1 teaspoon salt | 1 teaspoon honey |

Heat the fat in a stew pan and gently fry the pork for 5 minutes. Add the stock, leeks, parsley and salt. Stew gently for 10 minutes. Add the cooking apples and continue cooking. Meanwhile grind together the peppercorns, coriander seeds and mint. Add a few drops of vinegar, then the honey and a tablespoon of stock. Pour this mixture into the stew pan and cook until the meat is tender.

## PORK WITH APRICOTS

This is another medieval pork recipe which uses fruit. Here, dried apricots are used like sour apples to enhance the flavour of the pork. The acid in the fruit also makes the meat more digestible.

| | |
|---|---|
| pork dripping *or* butter *or* cooking oil | ½ pt (285 ml) stock |
| 1 onion, chopped | 4–6 peppercorns |
| 2 lb (900 g) loin of pork, cut in pieces | ½ teaspoon cumin seeds |
| | 1 teaspoon dried mint |
| 8 oz (225 g) dried apricots | 1 teaspoon salt |
| 1 cup wine | wine vinegar |
| | 1 teaspoon honey |

Heat the fat in a stew pan and fry the onion until transparent. Add the pork and fry gently together for 5 minutes. Add the apricots, wine and stock and stew gently. Meanwhile grind together the peppercorns, cumin, mint and salt. Moisten with a few drops of vinegar, the honey and a little stock. Mix together and add to the stew. Continue cooking until the meat is tender.

# PORK AND BEANS

This dish is somewhat like the cassoulet of southern France.

| | |
|---|---|
| 1 cup dried haricot beans | 8 oz (225 g) belly pork *or* |
| dripping *or* butter *or* cooking | thick bacon rashers, cut |
| oil for frying | in large pieces |
| 1 lb (450 g) lean pork, | 1 teaspoon basil |
| cut in cubes | 1 teaspoon thyme *or* sage |
| flour | freshly ground pepper |
| | salt to taste |
| | 1 pt (570 ml) stock |

Soak the beans overnight in water. Next morning strain them and leave to soak in fresh water until required. Preheat the oven to gas mark 2, 300°F (150°C). Heat the fat in a frying pan and gently fry the lean pork until lightly browned. Remove from the pan and roll in flour. Fry the belly pork for 2 minutes, then put it and any remaining fat in the bottom of a casserole. Drain the beans and put half of them on top of the bacon. Add the lean pork and sprinkle with the herbs, pepper and salt. Cover with the rest of the beans. Add just enough stock to cover everything. Put a well-fitting lid on the casserole and cook in the oven for 4 hours.

# PORK CHOPS WITH JUNIPER SAUCE

| | |
|---|---|
| dripping *or* butter *or* cooking | 2 bay leaves |
| oil for frying | 6 peppercorns |
| 1 onion, chopped | ½ pt (285 ml) dry cider |
| 6 pork chops | |

### *for the sauce*

| | |
|---|---|
| 1 oz (30 g) butter | 1 oz (30 g) flour |
| 1 clove of garlic, finely | 4 tablespoons yogurt |
| chopped | freshly ground pepper |
| 2 teaspoons juniper berries, | salt |
| crushed | |

Preheat the oven to gas mark 4, 350°F (180°C). Heat the fat in a pan and gently fry the onion until golden. Remove from the pan and keep warm. Put the chops in the pan and lightly brown on both sides, then remove them to a casserole dish and add the fried onions, the bay leaves, peppercorns and cider. Cover, and cook in the oven for 45 minutes.

Remove the chops from the casserole and keep them warm. Pour the stock into a jug or pan. Melt the butter for the sauce in a saucepan and gently fry the garlic and juniper until the garlic just begins to brown. Add the flour and stir well until smooth. Gradually pour in the stock and stir. Remove from the heat and stir in the yogurt. Add pepper and salt to taste. Put the chops back in the casserole dish and pour the sauce over them. Serve hot.

## STUFFED PORK

This recipe is adapted from a sixteenth-century one used when roasting joints of pork on a spit.

| | |
|---|---|
| 2 lb (900 g) joint of loin of pork | salt |
| | pinch of saffron |
| freshly ground pepper | 1 tablespoon milk |

*for the stuffing*

| | |
|---|---|
| 1 tablespoon pork dripping *or* butter *or* cooking oil | 4 oz (110 g) figs, chopped |
| | 4 oz (110 g) raisins |
| 1 small onion, finely chopped | 2 egg yolks |
| 1 teaspoon sage | ½ cup cream *or* yogurt |
| 1 teaspoon thyme | 6–8 oz (170–225 g) breadcrumbs |

butter
1 tablespoon flour
dry wine *or* cider

Preheat the oven to gas mark 4, 350°F (180°C). Cut the joint in half lengthwise and flatten each half with a wooden beater. Sprinkle with a little pepper and salt. Warm the milk and allow the saffron to dissolve in it.

Make the stuffing by heating the fat in a pan and gently frying the onion until transparent. Add the herbs and turn with the onion. Add the figs and raisins and fry together for 2 minutes. Turn off the heat. In a bowl, lightly beat the egg yolks into the cream. Stir in the saffron liquid. Add the breadcrumbs and the onion and dried fruit mixture. Stir together. Spread this stuffing mixture over one half of the loin. Put the other half on top and tie together with string. Smear with butter and put in a roasting tin. Cook in the oven for 1 hour, basting from time to time.

Use the roasting juices to make a gravy. First remove the joint to a serving dish, then pour the juice into a saucepan. Stir in the flour over a gentle heat, add the dry wine and stir until the gravy thickens.

# ROAST LEG OF PORK

| | |
|---|---|
| 1 leg of pork | juice of ½ lemon |
| butter *or* cooking oil | small bunch of sweet herbs |
| ½–1 bottle red wine | 1 tablespoon tomato puree |
| 2 anchovies, chopped | 1 tablespoon wine vinegar |
| yolks of 3 hard-boiled eggs | parsley sprigs |

Preheat the oven to gas mark 6, 400°F (200°C). If the skin of the joint has not been well scored by the butcher score it now with a sharp knife. Cut as much skin from the joint as you require for crackling. Place this on a separate shallow baking tray which has been lightly greased with butter or dripping, and put in the oven. Smear the joint with butter and put it in a roasting tin. Pour the wine over it and put in the oven. After 20 minutes, turn down the heat to gas mark 2, 300°F (150°C), and roast until the joint is well cooked. Allow about 25–30 minutes cooking time per 1 lb (450 g) weight. Baste the joint from time to time with the wine and meat juices. When cooked, remove the joint from the tin to a serving dish and keep warm. If the crackling is ready, turn down the oven to a warming heat. Pour the basting liquid into a pan and add the anchovies, egg yolks, lemon juice, herbs, tomato puree and vinegar. Boil together gently for 10 minutes. Strain, and serve the pork with this gravy poured over. Garnish with sprigs of parsley. Keep the crackling dry on a separate dish.

# PORK CUTLETS

| | |
|---|---|
| 1 lb (450 g) minced pork | freshly grated nutmeg |
| 2–4 cloves of garlic, finely chopped | freshly ground pepper |
| 1 tablespoon chives, chopped | 1 teaspoon salt |
| 1 teaspoon sage | 1 egg, beaten |
| 1 teaspoon thyme | breadcrumbs *or* flour |
| 1 teaspoon savory | cooking oil for frying |
| 1 teaspoon marjoram | chopped fresh parsley *or* watercress |
| 1 teaspoon grated lemon peel | lemon slices |

Mix together in a bowl the pork, garlic, herbs, lemon peel, nutmeg, pepper, salt and egg. Shape the mixture into small cutlets and roll in breadcrumbs or flour. Fry gently in oil until golden on both sides. Garnish with parsley or watercress and lemon slices. Serve with a tasty sauce or relish.

# BOILED HAM

In former times the cottager's and farmer's pig was killed before the winter to save the expense of winter feeding. The pig was then cut into joints which were salted to preserve them. Hams today contain far less salt, since only enough to make the ham is used. Such joints do not need to be steeped and boiled to remove excess salt. However, it is best to check this with your butcher.

| | |
|---|---|
| 3 lb (1·3 kg) boiling ham | 1 glass brandy *or* sherry |
| bunch of sweet herbs, including thyme | 1 glass red wine *or* dry cider |
| | honey |
| 4–10 cloves | butter |
| 2–4 bay leaves | 1 tablespoon chopped parsley |

Put the ham in a pan and add water to reach nearly the top of the meat. Throw in the herbs, cloves and bay leaves. Simmer gently on a low heat for 4 hours. Preheat the oven to gas mark 6, 400°F (200°C). Add the brandy and wine and continue cooking for a further 30 minutes. Remove the joint from the pan and smear it with honey and butter. Put on a baking tray and allow to brown for 20–30 minutes. Serve hot, sprinkled with parsley.

If gravy is required, make one by straining off some of the boiling liquid.

For a more decorative appearance, stick cloves into the fat just before baking. Score the fat with diagonal lines to make a diamond pattern, and push a clove into the middle of each diamond.

For an interesting stuffing, mix some apricot halves or pieces of apple with a tablespoon of ground almonds. Open the joint, install the stuffing and retie before boiling or baking.

# BAKED HAM WITH GREEN STUFFING

| | |
|---|---|
| 3 lb (1·3 kg) prime collar *or* neck chine of bacon | 2 tablespoons chopped fresh dandelion leaves |
| 2 tablespoons chopped parsley | 4–6 spring onions, chopped |
| 2 teaspoons thyme | freshly ground pepper |
| 2 teaspoons marjoram | butter *or* cooking oil |
| a few spinach leaves, chopped | honey |

Soak the joint beforehand if necessary (see note at the beginning of the previous recipe). Preheat the oven to gas mark 4, 350°F (180°C). To make the stuffing, mix together the herbs, spring onions and pepper. Open the joint and fill with the mixture. Tie up the joint with string. Smear with butter and wrap in foil. Put in a baking tin and cook for 1 hour. Remove the foil and spread the joint with a little honey. Allow to bake for a further 15–20 minutes without the foil.

# BACON WITH HERBS

Fried rashers of bacon, unknown in the rest of Europe, were a 'usual dish toward Shrovetide' in the fourteenth century, frequently served with fried eggs. The following recipe was still popular four centuries later. Use whatever quantities you find suitable. It allows plenty of scope for including other herbs, but take care that their flavour does not clash with that of the bacon. Chopped lamb's kidneys can be fried along with the bacon.

| | |
|---|---|
| spinach *or* cabbage | spring onions, chopped |
| dripping *or* butter *or* cooking oil | chopped fresh parsley |
| bacon rashers | |

Shred the spinach and cook in boiling water for 2 minutes. Allow to drain. Put a little fat in a frying pan and lightly fry the bacon. Add the spring onions and fry for a further 2 minutes. Remove from the pan and keep warm. Put in the greens and parsley and fry together. Arrange the greens and bacon on a serving dish.

# MEAT LOAF

| | |
|---|---|
| 1 lb (450 g) minced beef | 1 tablespoon chopped fresh |
| 1 lb (450 g) sausagemeat | parsley *or* coriander leaf |
| 1 onion, finely chopped | freshly ground pepper |
| 1–2 cloves of garlic, finely | salt |
| chopped | 1 egg, beaten |
| 1 teaspoon marjoram | 2 tablespoons breadcrumbs |
| 1 teaspoon sage | dripping *or* butter *or* cooking |
| freshly grated nutmeg | oil for greasing |

Preheat the oven to gas mark 4, 350°F (180°C). Mix all the ingredients together in a bowl except the egg and breadcrumbs. Grease a bread tin and put the meat mixture into it. Level the top with a spoon and brush with the beaten egg. Sprinkle the breadcrumbs on top. Bake in the oven for 45 minutes. Halfway through baking, remove the tin from the oven and carefully pour off any liquid. At the end of the baking pour off any more liquid that has formed. Serve hot with vegetables or cold with pickles and a salad.

## SPICY SAUSAGEMEAT

A medieval herb and spice mixture for use with sausagemeat would include peppercorns, cumin seeds, savory, rue, parsley and bay leaf as well as the usual sweet herbs.

| | |
|---|---|
| 1 lb (450 g) lean pork | 1 teaspoon salt |
| 1 cup breadcrumbs | ½ teaspoon powdered mace |
| 4 tablespoons milk | 1 teaspoon sage |
| 1–2 cloves of garlic, finely | 1 teaspoon thyme |
|   chopped | 1 teaspoon marjoram |
| 4 peppercorns | |
| 2 allspice berries | |

Cut the meat in pieces and mince finely. Moisten the breadcrumbs with warm milk and mix with the meat. Add the garlic. Grind the peppercorns and allspice together and mix with the salt and mace. Add the herbs. Wrap in clingfilm and keep for a day in a cool place or refrigerator so that the meat is aromatized. Next day make up into sausages or patties to be lightly fried in oil.

The sausagemeat could be wrapped in pastry to make a sausage roll, or mixed with small pieces of chicken or game to make a mixed meat pie.

## MEAT BALLS

This recipe is adapted from the medieval 'golden apples', in which saffron replaced the parsley.

| | |
|---|---|
| 1½ lb (680 g) lean pork *or* | 2 tablespoons currants |
|   beef | freshly grated nutmeg |
| 4 oz (110 g) breadcrumbs | freshly ground pepper |
| milk | salt |
| 1 small onion, finely chopped | 2 eggs, beaten |
| 1 tablespoon finely chopped | flour |
|   parsley | chopped fresh parsley |
| 1 teaspoon chopped fresh mint | lemon slices |

Cut the meat into pieces and mince finely. Moisten the breadcrumbs with a little warm milk or water. Squeeze the breadcrumbs and mix them in a bowl with the meat. Stir in the onion, parsley, mint, currants, nutmeg, pepper, salt and eggs. Leave to stand for 30 minutes. Shape the mixture into small balls and roll in flour. Thread onto a spit and barbecue the meat balls or lightly fry them in cooking oil until they are golden. Serve garnished with parsley and slices of lemon.

## WEST INDIAN PEPPER POT

Trade with the West Indies resulted in many exotic cargoes coming into the ports of the West Country. Just as sailors back from India brought with them a taste for curry, those who had visited the West Indies learned how to cook new dishes. By the time such recipes reached London, many of the exotic ingredients and spices had been dropped. Writing from the Temple Coffee House in 1788, Richard Briggs describes a traditional English stew of the time with the addition of allspice and chilli powder. As with all stews, you can vary the ingredients according to what is available.

| | |
|---|---|
| 1 lb (450 g) lean veal *or* beef brisket | 1 blade mace |
| 1½ lb (680 g) lean mutton | 2–4 dried red chillies |
| 8 oz (225 g) lean ham *or* gammon rashers | 4 peppercorns |
| 1 onion, chopped | 1 teaspoon salt |
| 2 carrots, chopped | 1 pt (570 ml) stock |
| 8 oz (225 g) turnips *or* swedes, chopped and cubed | 2–3 green bananas |
| small bunch of sweet herbs | 2 tablespoons dripping *or* butter *or* cooking oil |
| 2–4 allspice berries | 2 tablespoons flour |
| 4–6 cloves | 1 cup shelled prawns |
| | lime *or* lemon wedges |

Cut the meat and ham into small pieces. Put in a stew pan with the vegetables, herbs, spices and salt. Pour the stock over it and simmer gently for 1 hour, adding more water if necessary. Remove the meat from the pan. Meanwhile, boil the unpeeled green bananas in water in a separate pan until they are soft. Remove the skins and cut each banana into a few pieces. In another pan heat the fat and fry the meat pieces until lightly browned. Stir the flour into the meat and turn well. Put the meat back in the stew pan with the green bananas and prawns. Add a little more water or stock and stew for a further hour. Check seasoning and adjust if necessary before serving with wedges of lime or lemon.

## CHRISTMAS MINCEMEAT

People in the Middle Ages loved to eat meat mixed with fruit, a taste which was beginning to die out by the end of the eighteenth century. Here is a recipe which is one of the forerunners of today's very sweet mincemeat. 'It will keep six months . . . good to the East or West Indies' (Richard Briggs, *The English Art of Cookery*).

8 oz (225 g) best minced beef  
8 oz (225 g) apples, peeled, cored and chopped  
8 oz (225 g) currants  
4 oz (110 g) raisins *or* sultanas  
4 oz (110 g) almonds, blanched and chopped  
4 oz (110 g) shredded suet  
2 oz (60 g) soft brown sugar  
½ teaspoon powdered ginger  
½ teaspoon powdered cinnamon  
½ teaspoon freshly grated nutmeg  
2 cloves *and* 1 allspice berry, pounded together  
grated peel of 1 lemon  
juice of 1 lemon  
2 oz (60 g) candied peel  
2 tablespoons brandy *or* sherry  
¼ pt (140 ml) rum

Put all the ingredients in a bowl except the brandy and rum and mix well for 5–10 minutes. Add the brandy and rum and mix well again. Put the mixture into clean, dry jars or earthenware pots and seal well. Store in a cool, dry place.

Stir well before use. Put the mixture into pies – puff pastry is recommended – and cook as usual.

# STEWED LIVER

For a medieval variation of this recipe, stew the liver in wine and use thyme and lovage instead of sage. Tomatoes, undiscovered at that time, should of course be omitted.

1 lb (450 g) ox *or* sheep's liver, cut in slices  
dripping *or* butter *or* cooking oil for frying  
2 medium onions, sliced  
1 tablespoon flour  
grated nutmeg  
pinch of powdered mace  
freshly ground pepper  
½ teaspoon salt  
4 oz (110 g) bacon pieces *or* rashers, cut in pieces  
8 oz (225 g) chopped vegetables  
4 tomatoes, cut in four  
1 teaspoon sage  
1 pt (570 ml) stock

Put the liver in a bowl and pour boiling water onto it. Allow to steep for 15 minutes. Meanwhile heat the fat in a stew pan and gently fry the onion until transparent. On a plate, mix the flour with the seasoning. Drain the liver well and roll it in the seasoned flour. Add to the onions and turn well in the fat. Add the bacon pieces, vegetables, tomatoes and sage. Pour just enough stock into the pan to cover the ingredients. Put a lid on the pot and allow to stew gently for 1 hour.

## POOR MAN'S GOOSE

This is simply an economical hotpot or one-pot meal, made with liver (usually pig's liver), onions or leeks and potatoes. A more elaborate dish could be made by adding other vegetables such as carrots, cauliflower or swede.

| | |
|---|---|
| 1 lb (450 g) pig's *or* ox liver, cut in slices | 1 tablespoon flour |
| 1 lb (450 g) potatoes, parboiled and sliced | ½ teaspoon salt |
| | freshly ground pepper |
| dripping *or* butter *or* cooking oil for frying | sage |
| | 1 pt (570 ml) stock |
| 2 medium onions, sliced | 1 tablespoon chopped parsley |

Put the liver in a bowl and cover with boiling water. Allow to steep for 15 minutes. Preheat the oven to gas mark 3, 325°F (170°C). Put the potatoes on to boil but only allow them to half cook. Meanwhile, in a frying pan heat the fat and fry the onion for 2 minutes. Mix together on a plate the flour, salt and pepper. Roll the drained liver in the seasoned flour and put half in the bottom of a casserole dish. Spread over half of the fried onion and sprinkle with sage. Put in the rest of the liver and cover with the rest of the onion and more sage. Pour on enough stock to just cover the ingredients. Cover with a layer of sliced, parboiled potatoes. Cover the dish and bake in the oven for 1 hour, then remove the lid. Turn up the heat a little and allow the potatoes to brown for 30 minutes. Serve garnished with parsley.

## LIVER CUTLETS

This recipe is adapted from one by Hannah Glasse (see Bibliography).

| | |
|---|---|
| 8 oz (225 g) lamb's liver | 1 egg, beaten |
| 4–6 mushrooms, finely chopped | freshly ground pepper |
| 1 tablespoon finely chopped parsley | salt |
| | grated nutmeg |
| 1 small onion, finely chopped | breadcrumbs |
| | cooking oil for frying |
| 1–2 cloves of garlic, finely chopped | |
| 6 cloves, pounded | |
| 12 coriander seeds, pounded | |

Put the liver in a bowl and cover with boiling water. Allow to steep for 15 minutes. Drain and mince or cut finely. Put the liver in a bowl and add the mushrooms, parsley, onion, garlic, cloves, coriander and egg. Season with pepper, salt and nutmeg. Mix together well and shape into cutlets. Roll the cutlets in breadcrumbs and fry gently on both sides until golden.

## GRILLED STUFFED KIDNEYS

| | |
|---|---|
| lamb's kidneys, 2 per person | freshly ground pepper |
| chopped *or* ground almonds | butter |
| chopped parsley *or* | |
|   coriander leaf | |

Cut the kidneys almost in half and remove the skins. Snip out the white cores with kitchen scissors. Stuff with the almonds, parsley and pepper. Close up and smear with a little butter. Grill in the usual way or push together on a skewer to barbecue. Serve with bacon and fried onions.

## KIDNEYS IN PORT

| | |
|---|---|
| dripping *or* butter *or* cooking | ½ teaspoon powdered mace |
|   oil for frying | freshly ground pepper |
| 1 small onion, chopped | salt |
| 6 lamb's kidneys | ½ pt (285 ml) port |
| 1 tablespoon flour | |

Heat the fat in a large frying pan and gently fry the onion until transparent. Meanwhile, cut the kidneys in half, remove the skin and snip out the white cores with kitchen scissors. Put the kidneys in the pan and allow to brown a little. Shake the flour over them and stir well. Sprinkle with mace, pepper and salt. Pour the port into the pan and allow to simmer until the kidneys are tender (about 20 minutes). Serve with mushrooms and slices of lemon.

## STUFFED HEARTS

| | |
|---|---|
| 2–4 sheep's hearts | 1 medium onion, finely chopped |
| 8 oz (225 g) pork sausagemeat *or* | freshly ground pepper |
| minced pork | salt |
| 2 oz (60 g) breadcrumbs | 1 egg, beaten |
| 1 tablespoon chopped parsley | butter |
| 2 teaspoons marjoram | 1 cup red wine |
| 1 teaspoon sage | 1 cup water |
| 1 teaspoon thyme | 1 tablespoon flour |
| 1 teaspoon grated lemon peel | |

Wash the hearts and leave them to soak in water for 1 hour. Remove the clots of blood and the valves, then dry the hearts. Preheat the oven to gas mark 3, 325°F (170°C). Meanwhile mix the stuffing. In a bowl mix the sausagemeat, breadcrumbs, parsley, marjoram, sage, thyme, lemon peel, onion, pepper, salt and egg. Stuff the hearts with the stuffing mixture and smear with butter. Put them in a roasting tray. Pour in the wine and a cup of water. Roast in the oven until tender (about 2 hours). Make a gravy by adding the flour to the juice in the pan and stirring this over a gentle heat until it thickens.

## BRAISED TONGUE

| | |
|---|---|
| 3 sheep's tongues | 1 pint (570 ml) stock *or* water |
| dripping, butter *or* cooking | 4 cloves, pounded |
| oil for frying | ¼ teaspoon chilli powder |
| 1 onion, chopped | salt |
| 1 carrot, sliced | watercress |
| 1 small turnip *or* parsnip, cubed | 4 oz (110 g) mushrooms, lightly |
| small bunch of herbs | fried |

Leave the tongues in slightly salted water overnight. Drain them before use. The next day, heat the fat in a stew pan and gently fry the onion for 5 minutes. Add the sheep's tongues and turn them in the fat. Add the carrot, turnip or parsnip and herbs. Pour the stock or water into the pan and simmer gently for 3 hours. Remove the tongues and skin them by slitting the underside and peeling off the skin. Slice and return them to the pot. Add the cloves, chilli powder and salt to taste. Allow the tongue slices to stew for 15 minutes. Serve garnished with watercress sprigs and fried mushrooms.

This dish is excellent with new potatoes and peas and a relish such as mint sauce.

# TRIPE AND ONIONS

A traditional dish from the North which became popular in the nineteenth century as a cheap meal for the poorly paid industrial workers in the towns.

| | |
|---|---|
| 2 lb (900 g) dressed tripe | 2 oz (60 g) butter |
| 12–16 oz (340–450 g) onions, sliced | 1 oz (30 g) flour |
| | salt |
| 1½ pt (850 ml) milk | freshly ground pepper |
| small bunch of herbs | freshly grated nutmeg |

Wash the tripe and cut into 2 in (5 cm) squares. Put it in a pan and cover with water. Bring to the boil to blanch the tripe, then drain. Add the onions, milk and herbs and simmer until tender (1–1½ hours). Melt the butter in a saucepan, add the flour and stir for 3 minutes. Gradually add the milk from the tripe to make a sauce. Bring to the boil and season with salt, pepper and nutmeg. Keep stirring to prevent the sauce burning. Pour the sauce over the tripe and onions and allow to heat through. Serve hot with mashed potato.

# Poultry, Game & Wildfowl

By Roman times, ducks and geese as well as chickens had become domesticated in England. The turkey was a latecomer to the English diet and did not appear in recipes until the sixteenth century when it was brought over from the Americas. It has now taken the place of the goose as the main Christmas dish.

Today's demand for cheap poultry has meant that it has become difficult to obtain a flavourful and additive-free bird. The best product available on a wide scale is the chill-fresh bird. This has been carefully reared in stress-free conditions and is air-cooled after killing so that the flesh is allowed to mature and become flavoursome under natural, though controlled, conditions. Such a bird has pinkish rather than pasty or whitish flesh. You may, however, be lucky enough to have a reliable poulterer who can supply high-quality birds which have been carefully hung after killing and are only eviscerated at the point of purchase. It is recommended that you try to obtain either one of these two types of poultry.

Fresh poultry will keep for up to three days in a refrigerator. To store, remove the giblets if they are inside and keep separately. Put the bird on a plate with a loose covering.

For centuries, game and wildfowl have supplied a far greater part of the fleshmeat of the English countryman and woman than they do today. Recently these fresh foods have tended to become associated with the two extremes of shooting for sport and poaching. Sadly, the poacher who only killed to eat and respected the countryside is now part of country legend.

Follow the directions given in the recipes regarding storage for game and wildfowl.

*See also the recipes for:*

| | |
|---|---|
| Chicken Broth | Hare Soup |
| Chicken Paste | Potted Rabbit |
| Chicken Pie | Poultry Sauce |
| Giblet Soup | Rabbit Paste |
| Gipsy Pie | Squab Pie |
| | Venison Pie |

# ROAST CHICKEN WITH CHESTNUT STUFFING

| | |
|---|---|
| 12 oz (340 g) chestnuts | freshly ground pepper |
| 4–5 lb (1·8–2·3 kg) roasting chicken, including neck and giblets | grated nutmeg |
| | salt |
| | butter |
| 4 oz (110 g) bacon *or* ham | 6 rashers streaky bacon |
| small bunch of herbs | flour for dredging |
| ½ teaspoon powdered mace | lemon slices |

Roast the chestnuts or boil in water until soft. Allow to cool. Preheat the oven to gas mark 5, 375°F (190°C). Remove the neck and giblets from the chicken and place them in a pan. Cover with slightly salted water and boil gently until the liver is cooked. Wash the bird and dry it.

You should be able to make enough stuffing to fill the whole body cavity. Skin the chestnuts and mash them. Chop the cooked liver and heart, and the bacon or ham. In a bowl mix the chestnuts, liver, heart and bacon or ham with the herbs, spices and salt to taste. Mix together well, adding a little water or milk if necessary to bind. Push about one-third of the stuffing in through the neck and pull the flap of skin over it to cover. Put the rest of the stuffing in the body cavity. Smear the bird with butter and put it in a roasting tin. Sprinkle on a little salt and pepper. Lay the rashers of bacon over the breast and put the chicken in the oven. Allow about 20 minutes' cooking time per 1 lb (450 g) weight. Baste the bird from time to time with the juices in the pan. After 1 hour, take off the crispy bacon slices and keep them warm for serving later. About 15 minutes before the end of the cooking, turn up the heat to gas mark 7, 425°F (220°C). Dredge the breast with flour and baste well. This produces a nice crispy golden skin which enhances the appearance of the bird at the table. Serve garnished with slices of lemon.

It is essential that the bird should be cooked properly. Pierce the thickest part of the leg with a skewer. The juices that run out should be clear and golden, not pink. After removing the bird from the oven allow it to 'rest' for 10 minutes, which will make it easier to carve.

## ROAST CHICKEN WITH DATE STUFFING

This Roman recipe, still in use during the medieval period, is adapted here for modern use.

| | |
|---|---|
| 4–5 lb (1·8–2·3 kg) roasting chicken, including neck and giblets | 2 teaspoons lovage |
| | freshly ground pepper |
| | ½ teaspoon salt |
| 8 oz (225 g) dates, stoned | 1 teaspoon honey |
| 8 oz (225 g) hazelnuts, shelled and crushed | 1 tablespoon wine vinegar |
| | butter |
| 2 oz (60 g) breadcrumbs | ½ teaspoon mustard powder |
| 2 teaspoons mint | 1 cup wine |
| 1 teaspoon thyme | 1 tablespoon flour |

Preheat the oven to gas mark 5, 375°F (190°C). Put the neck and giblets in a small pan and cover with slightly salted water. Boil gently until the giblets are cooked. Wash the bird and dry it. In a bowl mix together the dates, nuts, breadcrumbs, herbs, pepper and salt. Add the honey and vinegar. Mix well and stuff the bird as in the previous recipe. Smear with butter and place in a roasting pan. Put the chicken in the oven and roast for 20 minutes per 1 lb (450 g) weight, basting frequently. Half an hour before the cooking is completed, chop the liver and heart. Stir the mustard into a cup of the giblet liquid and put it in a small pan with the liver and heart. Add the wine and simmer gently. Ten minutes before the bird is cooked, pour off the juices and add to the gravy. Thicken with flour and serve with the roast chicken.

# CHICKEN FRICASSEE

| | |
|---|---|
| 1 large chicken | 1 small onion, chopped |
| freshly ground pepper | 1 teaspoon thyme |
| salt | 1 teaspoon marjoram |
| 1 teaspoon grated lemon peel | ½ pt (285 ml) stock |
| 1–2 anchovies, chopped | 1 glass white wine |
| ½ teaspoon powdered mace | 1 tablespoon flour |
| ½ teaspoon grated nutmeg | yolks of 3 eggs |
| 2–4 cloves | 1 cup cream *or* milk *or* yogurt |

Cut the chicken into portion-sized pieces and remove the skin. Wash the pieces and dry them. Sprinkle with pepper and salt and put in a stew pan. Sprinkle over them the lemon peel, anchovies, mace, nutmeg, cloves, onion, thyme and marjoram. Pour the stock and wine into the pan. Stew gently (for 30–45 minutes) until the chicken is tender. Remove the chicken pieces. Stir the flour into the stewing liquid. Beat the egg yolks with the cream and mix into the sauce. Put the chicken pieces back in the pan and allow to simmer for 10 minutes. Do not allow the sauce to boil.

# CHICKEN WITH DRIED PEAS

This medieval recipe was originally brought to England by the Romans.

| | |
|---|---|
| 1 cup dried peas *or* beans | 2 tablespoons chopped parsley *or* coriander leaf |
| 1 large chicken | ½ pt (285 ml) stock |
| butter *or* cooking oil for frying | ½ pt (285 ml) wine |
| 1 onion, chopped | salt |
| freshly ground pepper | 2 tablespoons almonds, blanched and sliced |
| 2 teaspoons cumin powder | |

The day before, soak the dried peas in water. Next morning drain them. Put in a pan with fresh water and boil for 30 minutes. Discard the water. Add more water and continue boiling until the peas are nearly tender. Cut the chicken into portion-sized pieces. Heat the butter in a stew pan and fry the onion until transparent. Add the chicken pieces and sprinkle the pepper and cumin on top. Fry the chicken gently for 5 minutes. Sprinkle the parsley over it and add the drained, par-cooked peas. Pour on the stock and wine, and stew everything gently until the chicken and peas are fully cooked. Add salt to taste. Meanwhile fry the almonds and serve the chicken with this garnish.

# STEWED CHICKEN

| | |
|---|---|
| 1 large chicken | 1 onion, sliced |
| butter *or* cooking oil | 1 medium carrot, sliced |
| ¼–½ lemon, cut in pieces | 1 teaspoon salt |
| small bunch of herbs | 1 pt (570 ml) stock |
| 2–4 cloves | 1 glass white wine |
| 6 peppercorns | |

*for the sauce*

| | |
|---|---|
| 1 tablespoon ground | chopped celery tops |
| almonds *or* hazelnuts | a few mint leaves, chopped |
| 1 teaspoon lovage | |

Cut the chicken into portion-sized pieces and remove the skin. Smear the pieces with butter and put in a stew pan with the lemon, herbs, cloves, peppercorns, onion, carrot, salt, stock and wine. Stew gently until the chicken is tender.

To make the stewing liquid into a sauce strain it off into a saucepan. Add the nuts, lovage, celery tops and mint. Heat together for a few minutes and pour over the chicken.

# ROAST FOWL, SERVANT FASHION

The name of this eighteenth-century recipe indicates a rather less exotic stuffing for those eating 'below stairs'. Today, most people would be quite happy to eat in this 'servant fashion'.

| | |
|---|---|
| 4 lb (1·8 kg) chicken, | 1 egg, beaten |
| including neck and giblets | 1 tablespoon flour |
| 8 oz (225 g) breadcrumbs | 1 anchovy, chopped |
| 1 onion, chopped | a few capers *or* |
| 1 cup chopped parsley | nasturtium buds |
| freshly ground pepper | grated nutmeg |
| salt | |

Preheat the oven to gas mark 5, 375°F (190°C). Remove the neck and giblets from the chicken and boil in water until they are cooked. Take out the liver and heart and chop finely. Keep the giblet water. Put the chopped giblets in a bowl and add the breadcrumbs, onion, parsley, pepper and salt to taste. Stir in the egg and mix together well. Stuff the bird in the usual way. Smear it with butter and put it in a roasting tin. Put it in the oven and cook for 20 minutes per 1 lb (450 g) weight, basting from time to time. Twenty minutes before the bird is cooked, turn up the heat to gas mark 7, 425°F (220°C), to brown the outside.

Ten minutes before the end make up the gravy. Put the giblet water in a saucepan. Stir in the flour. Pour in some of the juice from the roasting tin. Add the anchovy, capers, salt and nutmeg and boil together gently until the gravy thickens. Serve with the chicken.

# ROAST TURKEY WITH MUSHROOM SAUCE

Turkeys are first recorded in England in 1541. In Georgian times a spiced bread sauce was preferred. Here is a more modern recipe, adapted from an eighteenth-century one. In those days the turkey was accompanied by tart sauces and oysters. For a 12–14 lb (5·4–6·4 kg) turkey you will need extra-wide foil.

*for the stuffing*

| | |
|---|---|
| 1 cup breadcrumbs | freshly ground pepper |
| 1 onion, finely chopped | salt |
| bunch of herbs, including sage | 6 oz (170 g) bacon, chopped |
| 4 oz (110 g) mushrooms, chopped | 1½ lb (680 g) pork sausagemeat |
| grated nutmeg | *or* minced pork |

butter
freshly ground pepper
8 bacon rashers

*for the sauce*

| | |
|---|---|
| butter | freshly ground pepper |
| 1 small onion, finely chopped | 2–4 lemon slices |
| grated nutmeg | 1 cup mushrooms, sliced |

Make the stuffing the day before you want to stuff the turkey. Put the breadcrumbs in a bowl and add enough hot water just to moisten them. Mix in the onion, herbs, mushrooms, nutmeg, pepper and salt to taste. Now add the bacon and sausagemeat, mix well and leave in a cool place overnight.

Next day, preheat the oven to gas mark 7, 425°F (220°C), just before stuffing the turkey. Put the stuffing in from both ends, as for a chicken. Lay large sheets of foil in the roasting tin, with enough overlap to come up to the top of the turkey and allow the edges to be folded together. Smear the turkey with butter and sprinkle pepper on top. Put the bird in the baking tin and lay rashers of bacon across the breast. Close up the foil to make a neat parcel and put it in the oven. Allow to cook for 30 minutes, then lower the heat to gas mark 3, 325°F (170°C), and cook for about 3 hours. Meanwhile put the giblets and neck in a pan and boil in slightly salted water for use as stock.

Remove the turkey from the oven and open up the foil. Roll down the sides to allow the breast to brown. Remove the bacon and keep the pieces warm. Baste well with the juices in the pan and return to the oven. Turn up the heat to gas mark 6, 400°F (200°C), and allow the turkey to complete cooking, basting it frequently. This will take 30 minutes–1 hour. Test for cooking by inserting a skewer in the thickest part of the leg. As for all birds, the juice should not be pink but clear and golden. The flesh should be beginning to fall away from the bone, with the joints loose. Allow the bird to 'rest' for 20 minutes before carving.

Meanwhile make the sauce. Heat a little butter in a frying pan and gently fry the onion until transparent. Sprinkle with nutmeg and pepper. Add the lemon slices and mushrooms and fry for 2 minutes. Add the stock from the boiled giblets and a cup of the juice from the roasted turkey. Allow to simmer together for 5 minutes. Serve with the turkey.

## ROAST DUCK WITH DAMSON SAUCE

Wild ducks and geese were plentiful in prehistoric times. Historical evidence suggests that they became domesticated during the Roman period. Fresh ducks are in season from August to February, and ducklings are available from February until August. They will keep for 5–6 days in cold weather. Choose a good heavy bird since ducks contain a lot of fat, much of which should drain out during the cooking and thus reduce the weight. For this reason no stuffing is required to keep the flesh moist, neither is it necessary to grease the bird before roasting.

| | |
|---|---|
| a 6 lb (2·7 kg) duck, including giblets | powdered ginger freshly ground pepper |
| 1 clove garlic, cut in half | salt |

*for the sauce*

| | |
|---|---|
| 1 small onion, finely chopped | 1 tablespoon wine vinegar |
| 1 teaspoon lovage | ½ teaspoon salt |
| 1 teaspoon powdered cumin | 1 tablespoon flour |
| 8 oz (225 g) damsons, stoned and halved | |

**sprigs of watercress**

Preheat the oven to gas mark 7, 425°F (220°C). Place the washed and dried bird in a roasting tin and pierce it all over with a skewer. This will allow the fat to run out during the cooking. Rub the duck all over with the clove of garlic. Sprinkle with ginger, pepper and a little salt. Put the bird in the oven and allow to cook for 20 minutes, then turn down the heat to gas mark 4, 350°F (180°C). Allow 30 minutes cooking time per 1 lb (450 g) weight. Look at the duck once or twice and pour off the accumulated fat. Do not baste. (Keep the fat for roasting other meats.)

Meanwhile boil the giblets in slightly salted water until cooked. Remove the liver and heart and chop finely. Strain off the stock. Put the chopped liver and heart and the strained stock into a separate pan. Add the onion, lovage, cumin, damsons, vinegar and salt. Stew together gently until the damsons are tender. Stir in the flour and cook until the sauce thickens. When the duck is cooked allow it to 'rest' for 5 minutes. Then cut in portions ready for serving. Put on a dish and pour the sauce over it. Garnish with watercress.

## ROAST GOOSE WITH FRUIT SAUCE

Geese are in season from September to February and goslings for the rest of the year. In the eighteenth century, the first geese of the season were eaten with a sauce made from green wheat and gooseberries. Nowadays the Michaelmas goose (29 September) is traditionally served with an apple sauce. Here is an Elizabethan recipe which includes 'My Lady's Sauce' made from a very tasty stuffing.

**a 10–12 lb (4·5–5·4 kg) goose, including giblets**

*for the stuffing*

| | |
|---|---|
| 8 oz (225 g) pears, peeled, cored and cut in pieces | small bunch of herbs, including sage |
| | freshly ground pepper |
| 2 quinces *or* apples, peeled, cored and cut in pieces | 1 teaspoon salt |
| | 1 teaspoon powdered ginger |
| 8 oz (225 g) grapes | 1 teaspoon salt |
| 2 cloves of garlic, finely chopped | 1 tablespoon flour |

*for the sauce*

| | |
|---|---|
| 1 small onion, finely chopped | grated nutmeg |
| 4 cloves, pounded | ½ pt (285 ml) dry wine |
| ½ teaspoon powdered mace | |

Put the giblets in a small pan and cover with slightly salted water. Boil until cooked. Remove the liver and heart and chop them finely. Keep the giblet stock. Preheat the oven to gas mark 7, 425°F (220°C).

To make the stuffing, put the chopped giblets, pears, quinces, grapes, garlic, herbs, pepper and salt into a large bowl and mix together well. Stuff the tail end of the goose and close with a skewer or sew up with thread. Put the goose in a roasting tin and prick it all over with a skewer to allow the excess fat to run out. Mix the ginger and salt with the flour and rub it all over the bird. Put it in the oven and roast for 30 minutes, then turn down the heat to gas mark 4, 350°F (180°C). Allow the goose to cook for 3–4 more hours. Pour off the excess fat from time to time. Do not baste. (The fat can be used for roasting potatoes.) Test the goose in the usual way by piercing with a skewer. The juice should be clear and golden, not pink. When the goose is cooked, remove it from the oven and turn the heat down to low. Take the stuffing out and keep it ready. Put the goose back in the oven while you make the sauce.

Heat a little goose fat and gently fry the onion in a large saucepan until it softens. Add the cooked stuffing. Sprinkle the cloves, mace and nutmeg on top. Add the giblet stock and wine and cook together over a gentle heat for 10 minutes. Cut the goose into portions and serve with the sauce poured over.

# ROAST STUFFED HARE

The flesh of hares and rabbits, like most meat, is flavoured by what the animal has fed on. Mountain rabbits will often be flavoured by aromatic herbs. Domestic rabbits have a more delicate flavour which is comparable with chicken. The flesh of hare is stronger in taste, darker in colour and coarser in texture. Rabbits are best bought in winter. Hares are in season from 15 August until the end of February. Rabbits and hares should be hung with the heads downwards, and skinned when needed for cooking.

**1 hare *or* large rabbit,
including giblets**

*for the stuffing*

| | |
|---|---|
| ½ cup breadcrumbs | 4–6 peppercorns |
| 1 tablespoon blanched | ½ teaspoon salt |
|   almonds, chopped | 1 egg, beaten |
| 1 tablespoon chopped walnuts | |

butter
freshly ground pepper
salt

Preheat the oven to gas mark 4, 350°F (180°C). Keep the liver, heart and kidneys of the hare and chop them. Make the stuffing by mixing the giblets in a bowl with the breadcrumbs, nuts, peppercorns, salt and egg. Stuff the belly and sew it up. Smear the hare with butter and sprinkle over it a little pepper and salt. Put in a roasting dish with the hind legs brought forward close to the body. Roast in the oven for 30 minutes per 1 lb (450 g) weight, basting from time to time. Serve with meat balls (see recipe in Meat chapter) and a sauce made with red wine.

# STEWED HARE

Many Easter traditions obviously predate the Christian festival in the same way that Yuletide predates Christmas. Easter is named after the Saxon goddess Eostre, and the Norse word *aust* for east – the place of sunrise, whose feast was at the vernal equinox. Her animal was the hare – now represented on Easter cards as a rabbit. The ingredients in this eighteenth-century recipe have undergone a slight change since a similar recipe of the 1680s. That recipe used white wine and the flavourings included thyme, parsley, bay leaf, grated orange peel, cloves, garlic and onion.

| | |
|---|---|
| 1 hare *or* large rabbit, cut in pieces | 1 anchovy, chopped |
| 1 onion, chopped | juice of ½ lemon |
| small bunch of savory | ¼ teaspoon chilli powder |
| 4 cloves | salt |
| 1 slice horseradish (optional) | 1 pt (570 ml)) stock |
| 2 blades mace | 1 glass red wine |
| | 1 tablespoon flour |

Put the hare in a stew pan. Sprinkle with the onion, savory, cloves, horseradish, mace, anchovy, lemon juice, chilli and salt to taste. Pour the stock and wine into the pan and stew gently for 2 hours, adding more liquid as necessary. The gravy can be thickened with flour before serving.

# JUGGED HARE

This method of cooking hare or rabbit began appearing in English printed recipe books in the 1720s. Originally the hare was cut in pieces and put in an earthenware pot or 'jug', which was suspended over a large pan or cauldron of boiling water. The jug was sealed and the meat cooked in a mixture of blood and herbs. Two hundred years later a recipe was sent to *Farmers' Weekly* from a woman in Suffolk – the ingredients were virtually unchanged from those in the eighteenth-century recipe given below.

| | |
|---|---|
| 1 hare *or* large rabbit, cut in pieces | 4 allspice berries |
| dripping *or* butter *or* cooking oil | 6 peppercorns |
| flour | 1 strip of lemon peel |
| small bunch of herbs | 1 teaspoon salt |
| 1 onion, stuck with 4 cloves | 1 pt (570 ml) stock |
| | 1 glass port |

Smear the hare pieces with fat and roll them in flour. Put them in a stew pan with the herbs, clove-onion, allspice, peppercorns, lemon peel and salt. Pour the stock over the meat, cover and simmer until the meat is tender (about 1½ hours). Remove the pan from the heat and pour off the liquid into a saucepan. Add the wine and thicken with a small knob of butter rolled in flour. Allow the gravy to simmer gently until it thickens. Return to the stew pan and reheat with the hare pieces. Serve with redcurrant jelly or a sauce.

## ROAST RABBIT

| | |
|---|---|
| 1 large rabbit *or* 2 smaller ones, including giblets | 1 teaspoon savory |
| | 1 teaspoon thyme |
| 2 tablespoons chopped, stoned dates | freshly ground pepper |
| | ½ teaspoon salt |
| 1 tablespoon raisins | dripping *or* butter *or* cooking oil |
| 1 small onion, chopped | 2 glasses red wine |
| 1 teaspoon rue | flour |

Clean the rabbit. Preheat the oven to gas mark 3, 325°F (170°C). Chop the liver, heart and kidneys and mix them in a bowl with the dates, raisins, onion, herbs, pepper and salt. Fill the belly of the rabbit and sew it up. Smear it all over with fat and put it in a roasting pan. Put it in the oven and roast for 1½–2 hours, basting from time to time.

To make a gravy, remove the rabbit from the oven. Open the belly and spoon the stuffing into the roasting juices. Add the wine and stir. Thicken with a little flour and simmer for a few minutes.

## RABBIT CASSEROLE

For a more medieval taste, use coriander leaf instead of parsley. Pound together peppercorns, lovage, cumin seed, coriander seed, mint, rue and a little raw onion. Add this to the cooking liquor with some honey and wine vinegar, and simmer until the onion is cooked.

| | |
|---|---|
| 1 rabbit, cut in pieces | small bunch of herbs |
| dripping *or* butter *or* cooking oil | freshly ground pepper |
| | salt |
| flour | 1 pt (570 ml) stock |
| 2 leeks, chopped | 2 teaspoons flour |
| 2 tablespoons chopped parsley | 1 orange, cut in slices |

Smear the rabbit pieces with fat and roll in flour. Put in a stew pan with the leeks, herbs, pepper and salt to taste. Add the stock, cover and simmer gently until the rabbit is tender (about 1 hour). Thicken the gravy with the 2 teaspoons of flour before serving. Garnish with slices of orange and serve with mushrooms.

## RABBIT STEW

| | |
|---|---|
| 1½ lb (680 g) rabbit pieces | 1 teaspoon powdered mace |
| bunch of sweet herbs, chopped | freshly ground pepper |
| ½ pt (285 ml) cider | salt |
| flour | 2 carrots, sliced and chopped |
| 2 tablespoons dripping *or* | 2 sticks celery, chopped |
| butter *or* cooking oil | 1 pt (570 ml) stock |
| 1 onion, chopped | |

Put the rabbit pieces in a bowl. Sprinkle them with the herbs and rub them into the meat. Pour the cider over them and marinate the rabbit overnight.

Next day, remove the rabbit pieces from the marinade and roll them in flour. Heat the fat in a stew pan and fry the onion until transparent. Add the rabbit pieces and fry for a few minutes until they begin to brown. Sprinkle on them the mace, pepper and salt to taste. Add the carrot and celery. Pour the rest of the marinade and stock into the pan. Allow to stew gently for 1–1½ hours until the meat and vegetables are tender.

## RABBIT WITH FORCEMEAT BALLS

| | |
|---|---|
| 6 prunes *or* dried apricots | 2 bacon rashers, chopped |
| 1 large rabbit, cut in pieces | small bunch of herbs |
| dripping *or* butter *or* cooking oil | freshly ground pepper |
| flour | salt |
| 1 onion, chopped | 1 pt (570 ml) stock |

*for the forcemeat*

| | |
|---|---|
| 8 oz (225 g) bacon, chopped | 1 cup breadcrumbs |
| finely *or* minced | 1 egg, beaten |
| 2 tablespoons finely chopped | freshly ground pepper |
| chives *or* spring onions | salt |
| 1 teaspoon marjoram | dripping *or* butter *or* cooking oil |
| 1 tablespoon finely chopped | |
| parsley | |

Soak the prunes overnight in water. Drain the following day. Wash and dry the rabbit. Heat the fat in a frying pan and lightly fry the rabbit pieces until they begin to brown. Roll the fried pieces in flour and put them in a stew pan. Add the prunes, onion, bacon, herbs, pepper and salt to taste. Add the stock, cover and simmer gently for 1½–2 hours.

Meanwhile make the forcemeat. In a bowl mix the bacon, chives, marjoram, parsley, breadcrumbs and beaten egg. Season with a little pepper and salt. Make the mixture up into small balls and fry in oil until golden. Serve with the cooked rabbit and gravy.

## ROAST VENISON

In Britain there are three main kinds of venison: red deer, fallow and roe deer. Many people consider the flesh of the English fallow deer to be the best. Buck venison is of better quality than doe and is in season from the end of June to the end of September. Doe is in season from October to the end of December. It is wise to check how long the venison has been hung – it should hang for about two weeks to relax the sinews. If you have to keep it yourself, wash the meat, dry and dust with pepper. Examine the meat every day, wipe dry and re-pepper. The quantities below are for a 9–10 lb (4–4·5 kg) joint.

A fruity sweet sauce has been served with venison since at least the first century AD, though today this sauce is often a more convenient commercial fruit jelly. Home-made sloe jelly or jam would be an ideal accompaniment. The recipe given here is for a medieval sauce.

*for the marinade*

| | |
|---|---|
| 1 bottle red wine | 3–4 bay leaves |
| 1 onion, chopped | 6–10 peppercorns |

butter
salt
freshly ground pepper
powdered cinnamon *or* ginger
6–10 fatty bacon rashers

*for the sauce*

| | |
|---|---|
| 8 oz (225 g) stoned dates | 4 cloves |
| 4 oz (110 g) dried apricots | small piece cinnamon |
| *or* damsons *or* prunes | |

Before roasting, marinate the meat for 2 days in red wine, laced with the onion, bay leaves and peppercorns. Keep the joint covered in a cool place. When you roast it, keep the marinade to make a gravy or sauce.

Preheat the oven to gas mark 3, 325°F (170°C). Smear the joint well with butter and sprinkle well with salt, pepper and powdered cinnamon or ginger. Lay it in a roasting tin and cover with bacon rashers. Put in the oven and roast for about 25 minutes per 1 lb (450 g) weight. Since venison can be a dry meat it is a good idea to wrap the joint in foil before roasting.

While the joint is cooking, put the marinade in a saucepan. Add the dates, apricots, cloves and cinnamon. Allow to simmer gently until the dried fruit is tender, adding more wine or stock if necessary. Serve the venison with the sauce poured over it.

## VENISON CASSEROLE

| | |
|---|---|
| 2 lb (900 g) venison | 1 teaspoon grated lemon peel |
| freshly ground pepper | small sprig of rosemary |
| dripping *or* butter *or* cooking oil | 2 medium carrots, sliced |
| 1 onion, chopped | ½ pt (285 ml) red wine |
| flour | ½ pt (285 ml) stock |
| 3 allspice berries | freshly ground pepper |
| 2 bay leaves | 1 teaspoon salt |
| 4–6 cloves | |

Make sure the venison has been well hung. Cut the meat into cubes and sprinkle with pepper. Preheat the oven to gas mark 2, 300°F (150°C). In a casserole dish, heat the fat and gently fry the onion until it begins to brown. Roll the meat in flour and add to the onion. Lightly brown the meat. Add the rest of the ingredients. Stir together, cover and simmer in the oven for 2 hours.

## ROAST WILD DUCK

There are many varieties of wild duck, which are in season from 1 August to 15 March. They should not be hung for more than a day. Draw when needed for use. Only young birds are suitable for roasting.

| | |
|---|---|
| 2 wild duck, dressed | 2 rashers bacon, chopped |
| 2 onions, each stuck with | juice of 2 oranges |
| 2 cloves | flour |
| 4 sprigs parsley | |
| 2 teaspoons marjoram | |

*for the sauce*

| | |
|---|---|
| 1 glass red wine | freshly ground pepper |
| 2 teaspoons flour | salt |

Preheat the oven to gas mark 6, 400°F (200°C). Put the onions inside the ducks with the herbs and chopped bacon. Lay the birds in a roasting tin and pour the orange juice over them. Rub them with flour and roast them in the oven for 30–40 minutes, basting from time to time. Remove the ducks from the tin and pour the juice into a saucepan. Add the wine. Thicken with flour and season with pepper and salt to taste. Simmer until the sauce thickens. Serve the duck with the sauce.

## PIGEON CASSEROLE

Game such as pigeon and rabbit formed a large part of the medieval cottager's diet. This was still true in the 1790s when this recipe was published, which is to this day a popular way of cooking pigeon in the West Country. Pigeons are in season all the year.

| | |
|---|---|
| 4 pigeons, dressed, but including giblets | salt |
| yolks of 2 hard-boiled eggs | dripping *or* butter *or* cooking oil |
| 1 tablespoon finely chopped parsley | small bunch of sweet herbs |
| 2 teaspoons grated lemon peel | 4 cloves |
| 1 cup breadcrumbs | 1 blade mace |
| grated nutmeg | 1 glass red wine |
| freshly ground pepper | 1 glass stock |
| | 1 lemon, cut in slices |

Wash and dry the pigeons. Boil the hearts and livers in water for 5 minutes. Remove and chop finely, keeping the giblet water for stock. Preheat the oven to gas mark 3, 325°F (170°C). Mix the giblets with the egg, parsley, lemon peel, breadcrumbs, nutmeg, pepper and salt to taste. Stuff the pigeons and smear each one with fat. Put in a casserole with the rest of the ingredients, cover and simmer in the oven for 1 hour. Serve garnished with lemon slices.

# Pies

Sing a song of sixpence
A pocketful of rye,
Four and twenty blackbirds
Baked in a pie.
When the pie was opened
The birds began to sing,
Wasn't that a dainty dish
To set before the king?

The word 'pie' begins to occur in fourteenth-century English, but its origins are obscure. Before that, birds, fish and pieces of meat were baked in pastry 'coffins'. Medieval pies could be colossal affairs containing a number of whole creatures, including live birds and frogs which would jump out when the pie was opened – to the delight of the guests!

*See also the recipe for:*
Apple Pie

## EEL PIE

| | |
|---|---|
| 2 eels | salt |
| 1 onion, sliced | 1 tablespoon flour |
| small bunch of herbs | juice of 1 lemon |
| 2 cups stock | 8 oz (225 g) shortcrust pastry |
| freshly ground pepper | 1 egg, beaten *or* a little milk |

Skin the eels (for instructions see the recipe for Stewed Eels) and cut into pieces. Put them in a pan with the fins, heads and tails. Add the onion, herbs, stock, pepper and salt to taste. Cook gently until the eel flesh comes away from the bones. Preheat the oven to gas mark 7, 425°F (220°C). Remove the eel pieces and put them in a pie dish. Sprinkle with flour and lemon juice. Add enough of the stewing stock just to cover the eels. Roll out the pastry. Damp the rim of the pie dish and press a strip of pastry round the edge. Place the pie crust on top of this. Damp the border and the cover and press together with the end of a fork. Trim with a knife. Brush the pastry with beaten egg to glaze. Pierce the centre to make a ventilation hole. Bake in the oven for 45 minutes.

## HERRING PIE

Medieval rents were often paid in eel or herring pies. The City of Norwich rendered twenty-four herring pies annually to the king, each pie containing five herrings flavoured with spices.

| | |
|---|---|
| 5 herrings | freshly ground pepper |
| butter | salt |
| 1 lb (450 g) shortcrust pastry | 2 apples, peeled, cored and sliced |
| powdered mace | 1 onion, sliced |
| 2 cloves, ground | ½ pt (285 ml) stock |

Preheat the oven to gas mark 5, 375°F (190°C). Scale, gut and wash the herrings. Cut off the heads, fins and tails. Smear a pie dish with butter. Divide the pastry in half, and roll out one half to line the pie dish. Smear the pastry with a little more butter and put in the herrings. Season with mace, cloves, pepper and salt. Lay the apple slices over the fish, then the onion. Pour the stock over them. Roll out the rest of the pastry and cover the dish with it. Trim the edges with a knife. Bake in the oven for 1½ hours.

# FLOUNDER PIE

This recipe, collected by Richard Briggs in the 1780s, is suitable for most flat fish.

| | |
|---|---|
| 2–4 flounders | powdered mace |
| butter | freshly ground pepper |
| 1 lb (450 g) shortcrust | salt |
| pastry | |

*for the stock*

| | |
|---|---|
| 1 pt (570 ml) water | ½ teaspoon salt |
| 1 sprig parsley | ½ glass white wine |
| 1 strip lemon peel | |

Gut, wash and dry the fish. Cut the meat from the bones and fins (for instructions see the recipe for Fried Plaice). Smear the pie dish with butter. Divide the pastry in half, and roll out one half to line the pie dish. Smear the pastry with a little more butter and lay the fish slices on top. Season with mace, pepper and salt. Preheat the oven to gas mark 5, 375°F (190°C). Put the bones in a pan with the water. Add the parsley, lemon peel, salt and wine. Boil until the stock is reduced to about half. Strain and allow to cool. Pour the stock over the fish. Cover with the rest of the pastry, trimming the edges with a knife, and bake in the oven for 1½ hours.

# FISH PIE

From the Middle Ages onwards hot or cold fish pies were eaten. The pastry 'coffin' or 'shell' was regarded as a means of cooking the fish, and was not always eaten. Often, when the pie was opened, the juices would be poured out and mixed with wine and spices to be spooned onto warm bread. In this modern recipe, potato replaces the piecrust. There is no juice so a suitable sauce is required (see the Sauces chapter).

| | |
|---|---|
| 1½ lb (680 g) haddock | 1½ lb (680 g) potatoes |
| 1 small onion, chopped | powdered mace |
| 1 sprig parsley | 1 tablespoon flour |
| freshly ground pepper | 1–2 anchovies, chopped |
| salt | 2 tablespoons melted butter |

Cut the fish in pieces and put in a stew pan. Add the onion, parsley, pepper and salt to season. Cover with water and simmer gently until the fish is tender (15–20 minutes). Meanwhile, put the potatoes on to boil. Mash when soft. Preheat the oven to gas mark 4, 350°F (180°C). When the fish is cooked remove it but keep the stock. Flake the fish and put in an ovenproof dish. Sprinkle with mace, flour and anchovy. Pour the butter over it. Spread the mashed potato over the fish like a piecrust. Bake in the oven until golden brown on top (about 30 minutes).

## LENTEN FISH PIE

In earlier centuries fish was an acceptable food during Lent. Here is a medieval recipe for a pie which was made to mark the middle of Lent. A large pie dish is required. By the seventeenth century, the dates given here had been replaced by a sprinkling of sugar – now freely available from the West Indies.

| | |
|---|---|
| 1 lb (450 g) haddock | a few bay leaves |
| 1 lb (450 g) cod | 4 peppercorns |
| a few figs, halved | 1 blade mace |
| ½ cup raisins | 1 teaspoon salt |
| 1 lb (450 g) apples, peeled, cored and sliced | 1 glass wine |
| | butter |
| 1 lb (450 g) pears, peeled, cored and sliced | 1 lb (450 g) shortcrust pastry |
| | dates, stoned and halved |
| 2 tablespoons finely chopped parsley | |

Cut the fish in pieces and put in a stew pan with the fruit. Sprinkle with the herbs, spices and salt. Add the wine and enough water to cover. Simmer gently until the fish is just tender. Preheat the oven to gas mark 5, 375°F (190°C). Grease a pie dish with butter and line with half the pastry. Fill the dish with the stewed ingredients and cover with the rest of the pastry, trimming the edges with a knife. Bake in the oven until the crust is nice and golden (about 30 minutes). Serve garnished with dates.

## VEAL PIE

| | |
|---|---|
| 1½ lb (680 g) veal | salt |
| flour | 4 oz (110 g) stoned dates |
| small bunch of herbs | 8 oz (225 g) plums, stoned and halved |
| grated nutmeg | |
| small piece of cinnamon | 1 glass white wine |
| freshly ground pepper | 8 oz (225 g) shortcrust pastry |

Trim the veal and cut in cubes. Put in a pan and just cover with water. Allow to boil for 20 minutes. Preheat the oven to gas mark 4, 350°F (180°C). Remove the veal and roll it in flour, then put it in a pie dish. Sprinkle with the herbs, spices and salt to taste. Add the fruit. Pour in the wine and cover with a piecrust, trimming the edges with a knife. Bake in the oven for about 30 minutes.

## STEAK AND KIDNEY PIE

Baby and I
Were baked in a pie,
The gravy was wonderful hot.
We had nothing to pay
To the baker that day
And so we crept out of the pot.

| | |
|---|---|
| 8 oz (225 g) steak | small bunch of herbs |
| 8 oz (225 g) kidney | freshly grated nutmeg |
| dripping *or* butter *or* cooking oil | freshly ground pepper |
| 1 onion, chopped | salt |
| 1 tablespoon flour | 4 oz (110 g) mushrooms, sliced |
| 8 oz (225 g) tomatoes, cut in | ½ pt (285 ml) stock |
| quarters | 1 lb (450 g) suet crust pastry |

Trim the steak and kidney and cut in cubes. In a pan, heat the fat and gently fry the onion until transparent. Add the steak and kidney and lightly fry together. Add the flour and mix together. Add the tomatoes, herbs, spices and salt to taste. Add the mushrooms, then pour in the stock. Allow to simmer gently until the meat is tender (1½–2 hours). Pour into the pie dish. Preheat the oven to gas mark 7, 425°F (220°C). Roll out the pastry, but not as thin as shortcrust. Cut a strip of pastry as wide as the edge of the dish. Dampen the edge and press on the strip. Dampen the strip and press on the pie crust. Seal the edges by pressing with a fork, and trim the edges with a knife. Use any leftover pastry to make decorations on the piecrust. Pierce the centre to allow steam to escape. Bake in the oven until the pastry is golden (30–40 minutes).

# LAMB PIE

This is perhaps the forerunner of the shepherd's pie. The suet pastry may be replaced by parboiled, sliced or mashed potato.

| | |
|---|---|
| 1 lb (450 g) lamb fillet | freshly ground pepper |
| 2 sheep's kidneys | salt |
| dripping *or* butter *or* cooking oil | 1 lb (450 g) leeks, sliced |
| 1 onion, sliced | 1 cup wine |
| 1 tablespoon flour | 1 cup stock |
| 1 teaspoon thyme | 1 lb (450 g) suet crust pastry |
| 1 teaspoon rosemary | |

Trim the lamb and kidneys and cut in cubes. Heat a little fat in a pan and lightly fry the onion until transparent. Add the lamb and kidney and allow to brown lightly. Put them all in the bottom of a pie dish and sprinkle with flour, the herbs, and pepper and salt to taste. Cover with the sliced leeks. Pour the stock on top. Preheat the oven to gas mark 7, 425°F (220°C). Roll out the pastry, but not as thin as for shortcrust. Cut a strip of pastry as wide as the edge of the dish. Dampen the edge and press on the strip. Dampen the strip and press on the piecrust. Seal by pressing down with a fork, and trim the edges with a knife. Use any leftover pastry to make decorations for the piecrust. Pierce the centre to allow the steam to escape. Bake in the oven until the pastry is golden (30–40 minutes).

# SWEET LAMB PIE

This is adapted from an eighteenth-century recipe. To make a sweet lamb pie in the Cumbrian style, add a glass of rum to the ingredients. The crust may be of puff or shortcrust pastry.

| | |
|---|---|
| 8 oz (225 g) pork sausages | 1 tablespoon raisins *or* sultanas |
| 8 oz (225 g) trimmed lamb | 4–6 plums |
| 8 oz (225 g) trimmed pork | 1 lb (450 g) potatoes |
| salt | 1 tablespoon chopped candied |
| freshly ground pepper | peel |
| powdered mace | 1 tablespoon melted butter *or* |
| grated nutmeg | cooking oil |
| 4 cloves, pounded | 8 oz (225 g) shortcrust pastry |

Slice the sausages and cut up the meat in small pieces. Put them in a pie dish. Sprinkle with salt, pepper, mace, nutmeg and ground cloves. Sprinkle with raisins. Slice the plums and add to the dish. Meanwhile, boil the potatoes until almost cooked, and then slice. Put a layer of potato into the dish and sprinkle with salt, pepper, mace and candied peel. Pour the melted butter over. Preheat the oven to gas mark 5, 375°F (190°C). Cover with a pastry lid, trimming the edges with a knife, and bake in the oven until the pastry is golden (about 45 minutes). Serve with a hot gravy.

## SPICY MUTTON PIE

This sixteenth-century recipe is a direct descendant of the medieval meat pies which were well spiced and sweetened with fruit. It is adapted from one in *The Good Hous-Wives Treasurie* (1588).

| | |
|---|---|
| 1 lb (450 g) mutton *or* lamb | 1 tablespoon currants |
| dripping *or* butter *or* cooking oil | 1 cup stoned dates *or* stoned plums |
| 1 tablespoon flour | grated nutmeg |
| 2 eggs, hard-boiled and chopped | ½ teaspoon powdered mace |
| 1 tablespoon rosewater | freshly ground pepper |
| juice of 1 orange | 1 cup stock |
| 1 teaspoon grated lemon peel | salt |
| 2 cloves | 8 oz (225 g) shortcrust pastry |

Mince the meat. Heat a little fat in a pan and add the mince. Allow to brown gently for 5 minutes. Add the flour and stir together over the heat for 2 minutes. Remove from the heat. Mix in the eggs, rosewater, orange juice, lemon peel, cloves, currants and dates. Put all these ingredients in a pie dish. Sprinkle with nutmeg, mace and pepper. Add the stock. Sprinkle with a little salt to taste. Preheat the oven to gas mark 7, 425°F (220°C). Roll out the pastry and cover the pie dish, trimming the edges with a knife. Pierce the centre to allow the steam to escape. Bake in the oven until the crust is golden (about 30 minutes).

# SQUAB PIE

The old word for a young unfledged bird or pigeon is still used to describe this West Country pie. Once made with pigeons, it is now usually made with mutton. Essential ingredients are apples and onions. The pie can be served the Devon way, with thick cream. In the fidget pie of Huntingdon and Cambridge, the meat ingredient is bacon or ham.

| | |
|---|---|
| 1½ lb (680 g) mutton *or* lamb *or* other meat | salt |
| small bunch of herbs, including rosemary | 1 onion, chopped |
| | 2 apples, peeled, cored and sliced |
| 1 teaspoon grated lemon peel | 1 large potato, sliced |
| grated nutmeg | ½ pt (285 ml) stock |
| ½ teaspoon powdered mace | 8 oz (225 g) shortcrust pastry |
| freshly ground pepper | milk |

Trim the meat and cut into small pieces. Sprinkle with the herbs, lemon peel, nutmeg, mace, pepper and salt to taste. Put in a bowl and mix in the onion, apple and potato. Place in a pie dish and pour the stock over. Preheat the oven to gas mark 4, 350°F (180°C). Roll out the pastry. Dampen the edges of the pie dish and put on the piecrust. Seal the edges with a fork and trim off with a knife. Pierce the centre to allow steam to escape. Brush the pastry with a little milk to glaze. Put in the oven to bake for 1½–2 hours until the pastry is golden.

# PORK PIE

Up to the 1900s, pork was the main meat of modest country families, with beef and mutton eaten fresh on festive occasions. Pig-killing was an important autumn event, and a huge range of cuts and dishes was created. At market, pork pies wore sprigs of sage and mutton pies sprigs of mint to distinguish them as well as to indicate their seasoning.

This is the traditional pork pie to be found in numerous eighteenth-century cookery books including those of Glasse, Mason, Farley and Cole. It in no way resembles the small commercial pie which is filled with fat and jelly along with a selection of chemical additives. There are a number of opinions about the best pastry for raised pies. Shortcrust would suit this recipe, but described below is a traditional raised crust pastry which goes particularly well with the meat. The cooking produces two kinds of texture while the pie is hot – a crisp piecrust and a softer edge. This recipe works perfectly if you put the pastry inside a small cake tin with a removable base.

| | |
|---|---|
| 1½ lb (680 g) pork shoulder *or* lean pork | ¾ pt (425 ml) water |
| 1 cup wine | salt |
| 12 oz (340 g) apples, peeled, cored and sliced | 12 oz (340 g) flour |
| 3 oz (85 g) lard *or* pure dripping | chopped fresh sage |
| | freshly ground pepper |
| | grated nutmeg |
| | 1 egg, beaten |

### for the gravy

| | |
|---|---|
| 1 pt (570 ml) stock | 1–2 teaspoons anchovy essence *or* chopped anchovy |
| 1 teaspoon rosemary | 1 teaspoon flour |

Cut the pork into small pieces, and trim off the excess fat and gristle. Put the meat in a bowl and marinate in the wine for 2–3 hours. Prepare the apples.

To make the raised crust pastry, heat in a saucepan the fat, water and a pinch of salt. Bring to the boil. Sift the flour into a mixing bowl and pour in the hot liquid gradually, mixing with a knife, until a stiff dough is formed. You may not need all of the boiled liquid. Grease the bottom and sides of the cake tin. Cut off a quarter of the dough for the lid. Form the rest of the dough into a flat cake and lay it in the bottom of the tin. Press down to form the base of the pie and work the dough up the sides of the tin. You now have a pastry container for the pie ingredients.

Preheat the oven to gas mark 6, 400°F (200°C). Drain the wine from the pork and keep for making the gravy later on. Put a layer of pork in the bottom of the pie. Sprinkle with sage, pepper, nutmeg and salt. Put on a layer of apple slices. Keep adding layers of pork, then seasoning, then apple until the ingredients are used up. Finish with a dome shape. Flatten the last quarter of pastry to make a lid. Moisten the edges and press the lid on. Trim with a knife and use the trimmings to form a decoration on top. Seal the edges with the prongs of a fork. Pierce the crust to allow the steam to escape. Brush with egg to glaze.

Put the pie in the oven and bake for 30 minutes. Turn down the heat and bake for a further 1½ hours. Let the pie 'rest' for 10 minutes before you remove it from the cake tin.

Make a gravy from the wine and stock. Add rosemary and anchovy essence and boil it all together. Mix the flour with a little stock in a cup and pour in. Serve when the gravy has thickened.

## MEDLEY PIE

| | |
|---|---|
| 12 oz (340 g) boiled ham *or* bacon | powdered ginger |
| 12 oz (340 g) cold cooked meat | freshly ground pepper |
| 1½ lb (680 g) apples, peeled, cored and sliced | salt |
| small bunch of herbs | 1 cup ale *or* cider |
| | 8 oz (225 g) shortcrust pastry |
| | 1 egg, beaten |

Cut the bacon and meat into small pieces. Put half in the bottom of a pie dish. Season with the herbs, ginger, pepper and salt to taste. Cover with half the apple slices. Put in the rest of the meat, season and cover with the rest of the apple. Add the ale. Preheat the oven to gas mark 5, 375°F (190°C). Roll out the pastry. Dampen the edges of the pie dish and cover with the piecrust. Seal the edges with a fork and trim with a knife. Glaze by brushing with egg. Pierce the centre to allow the steam to escape. Bake in the oven for 1–1½ hours.

## KIDNEY PIE

For an Elizabethan taste to this dish, substitute dates and raisins for the celery.

| | |
|---|---|
| 2 large sheep's kidneys | 2 sticks celery, chopped |
| 1 teaspoon rue | 4 hard-boiled eggs, sliced |
| 1 teaspoon thyme | ½ cup breadcrumbs |
| 4 cloves | 1 cup red wine |
| grated nutmeg | 8 oz (225 g) shortcrust pastry |
| freshly ground pepper | |
| salt | milk |

Chop the kidneys. Put them in a pie dish and season with the herbs, spices and salt to taste. Add the celery, eggs and breadcrumbs. Pour the wine over. Preheat the oven to gas mark 4, 350°F (180°C). Roll out the pastry. Dampen the edges of the pie dish and cover with the piecrust. Seal with a fork and trim with a knife. Glaze with a little milk and pierce the centre to allow the steam to escape. Bake in the oven for 2 hours.

# HUMBLE PIE

In the seventeenth century deer offal was known as 'numbles'. Out of this a numble pie was made. This term soon became corrupted to an 'umble' or 'humble' pie. 'To eat humble pie' is a colourful phrase, since the nearest the poor folk of the time would have come to eating deer would have been the offal rather than the venison itself.

| | |
|---|---|
| 1½ lb (680 g) deer offal (heart, kidneys, liver) *or* offal from another animal | ½ teaspoon powdered mace |
| | ½ teaspoon powdered ginger |
| | freshly ground pepper |
| ½ cup shredded suet | salt |
| 1 tablespoon flour | ½ pt (285 ml) wine |
| ½ cup currants | ½ pt (285 ml) stock |
| 2 tablespoons chopped parsley | 1 lb (450 g) shortcrust pastry |
| sprig of rosemary | 1 egg, beaten |
| a few bay leaves | |

Chop the offal. Put it in a bowl with the suet, flour and currants and mix together. Season with the herbs, spices and salt to taste. Put this mixture in a pie dish and pour the wine and stock over it. Preheat the oven to gas mark 4, 350°F (180°C). Roll out the pastry. Dampen the edge of the pie dish and cover with the piecrust. Seal with a fork and trim with a knife. Brush with egg to glaze. Pierce the centre to allow the steam to escape. Bake in the oven for 2 hours.

# CHICKEN PIE

At Sussex weddings the couple's fertility and prosperity was ensured by the 'bride's pie' – a hen, filled with hard-boiled eggs, in a thick pastry crust.

| | |
|---|---|
| 1½ lb (680 g) chicken | 1 blade mace |
| dripping *or* butter *or* cooking oil | 4–6 peppercorns |
| 1 onion, chopped | salt |
| 2 sticks celery, chopped | 2 tablespoons chopped parsley |
| 2 hard-boiled eggs, sliced | ½ pt (285 ml) stock |
| small bunch of herbs, including thyme | ½ pt (285 ml) white wine |
| | 1 lb (450 g) shortcrust pastry |

Cut the chicken into pieces. Heat the fat in a pan and lightly fry the onion until transparent. Add the chicken pieces and turn them in the fat for 5 minutes. Put into a pie dish. Add the celery, eggs, herbs, spices and salt to taste. Sprinkle with parsley. Pour the stock and wine over the top. Preheat the oven to gas mark 6, 400°F (200°C). Roll out the pastry. Cut a strip as wide as the edge of the dish. Dampen the edge of the dish and press on the pastry strip. Dampen the strip and cover with the piecrust. Seal the edge with a fork, and trim with a knife. Extra pieces of pastry can be used to make leaf-shaped decorations which are fixed to the piecrust. Bake in the oven until the pastry is well browned (1–1½ hours).

## GIPSY PIE

This is a poacher's version of the traditional game pie. Simply use whatever game you have available to make a tasty pie.

| | |
|---|---|
| 1 young rabbit | freshly ground pepper |
| 8 oz (225 g) any available meat | salt |
| 2 pork sausages | ¾ pt (425 ml) stock *or* cider |
| flour | 8 oz (225 g) shortcrust pastry |
| bunch of herbs | |

Soak the skinned and gutted rabbit in cold salted water for 1–2 hours. Wipe it dry and cut into pieces. Cut the meat and sausages into pieces. Roll all the meat and sausage pieces in flour and put them in a pie dish. Sprinkle over them the herbs, pepper and salt to taste. Add the stock or cider. Preheat the oven to gas mark 4, 350°F (180°C). Roll out the pastry. Dampen the edges of the pie dish and cover with the piecrust. Seal the edges with a fork and trim with a knife. Pierce the centre to allow the steam to escape. Bake in the oven for 1½–2 hours until the pastry is golden.

# VENISON PIE

Use the cheaper cuts of venison for this dish.

| | |
|---|---|
| 1 lb (450 g) venison, well hung | ½ pt (285 ml) red wine |
| 1 onion, chopped | ½ pt (285 ml) stock |
| bunch of herbs, including bay leaf | 1 lb (450 g) shortcrust pastry |
| freshly ground pepper | 1 egg, beaten |
| salt | |

Cut the venison in small pieces. Put them in a pan with the onion, herbs, pepper and salt to taste. Add the red wine and stock and simmer gently until the meat is tender. Pour into a pie dish with as much of the stewing liquor as necessary. Preheat the oven to gas mark 6, 400°F (200°C). Roll out the pastry. Cut a strip as wide as the edge of the pie dish. Dampen the edge and press on the pastry strip. Dampen the strip and cover with the piecrust. Press to seal with a fork, and trim with a knife. Use the trimmings to make a nice leaf pattern on the piecrust. Brush with the egg to glaze. Pierce the centre to allow the steam to escape. Bake in the oven for 1 hour. Serve with gooseberry sauce or venison sauce (see the Sauce chapter).

# LENT MINCE PIE

This eighteenth-century recipe was popular during the fasting time of Lent when meat-eating was forbidden. It makes a tasty break in the monotony of a bland fasting regime.

| | |
|---|---|
| 6 hard-boiled eggs, chopped | grated nutmeg |
| 6 apples, peeled, cored and chopped | 1 teaspoon salt |
| 1 cup raisins | 1 small glass brandy *or* sherry |
| 1 tablespoon candied peel | 1 glass wine |
| 2 cloves | butter |
| ½ teaspoon powdered mace | 1 lb (450 g) puff pastry |
| ½ teaspoon powdered ginger | juice of 1 orange |

In a bowl, mix together the eggs, apples, raisins, candied peel, cloves, mace, ginger, nutmeg and salt. Pour over them the brandy and wine. Preheat the oven to gas mark 7, 425°F (220°C). Roll out the pastry. Grease a pie dish and line with half of the pastry. Pour in the filling mixture. Sprinkle with the orange juice and cover with the piecrust made from the other half of the pastry. Seal and trim the edges. Pierce the centre to allow the steam to escape. Bake in the oven until the pastry is golden (about 1 hour).

# MUSHROOM PIE

| | |
|---|---|
| 1 lb (450 g) shortcrust *or* puff pastry | sage |
| butter | grated nutmeg |
| 12 oz (340 g) mushrooms, sliced | freshly ground pepper |
| 2 rashers bacon, chopped | ½ pt (285 ml) stock |
| small bunch of herbs, including | milk |

Divide the pastry in half. Preheat the oven to gas mark 7, 425°F (220°C). Smear the pie dish with butter. Roll out half the pastry and line the dish with it. Put in the mushrooms. Sprinkle with the bacon, herbs and spices. Pour the stock over the top. Roll out the rest of the pastry and cover the dish. Press the edge with a fork to seal, and trim with a knife. Pierce the centre to allow the steam to escape. Brush with milk to glaze. Bake in the oven until the pastry is golden (about 1 hour).

# PUMPKIN PIE

| | |
|---|---|
| butter | 2 allspice berries, pounded |
| 8 oz–1 lb (225–450 g) shortcrust pastry | grated nutmeg |
| | salt |
| 3 eggs | 1 lb (450 g) pumpkin, peeled |
| 2–4 oz (60–110 g) sugar | and cut in cubes |

If you use 1 lb (450 g) pastry you can make a base to the pie as well as a lid. Grease a pie dish with butter and roll out the pastry. Use half to line the dish. Preheat the oven to gas mark 6, 400°F (200°C). Beat together the eggs, sugar, spices and salt to taste. Put the pumpkin in the pie dish and pour the egg mixture over it. Cover with the rest of the piecrust. Seal the edges, trim, and pierce the centre to allow the steam to escape. Bake in the oven until the pastry is golden (40 minutes–1 hour).

## ONION PIE

butter
1 lb (450 g) puff *or* shortcrust
  pastry
8 oz (225 g) potatoes, parboiled
1 lb (450 g) onions, sliced
8 oz (225 g) apples, peeled, cored
  and sliced

2 eggs, hard-boiled and sliced
powdered mace
freshly ground pepper
salt
1 tablespoon chopped parsley
½ pt (285 ml) white wine
milk

Smear a pie dish with butter. Roll out half the pastry and line the pie dish. Slice the potatoes and add them in a layer, followed by a layer of onions, apples and eggs. Sprinkle with mace, pepper and salt. Put in any remaining ingredients and season again. Sprinkle with parsley. Pour in the wine. Preheat the oven to gas mark 7, 425°F (220°C). Roll out the rest of the pastry for the piecrust lid, press on and trim. Pierce the centre to allow the steam to escape. Brush with milk to glaze. Bake in the oven until the pastry is golden (about 1 hour). Serve with thick cream, curd cheese or yogurt.

## LEEK PIE

2 lb (900 g) leeks
small bunch of herbs,
  including bay leaf
1 pt (570 ml) water
2 rashers bacon, chopped
2 eggs

¼ pt (140 ml) cream *or* yogurt
grated nutmeg
freshly ground pepper
salt
8 oz (225 g) puff pastry
milk

Clean and trim the leeks and chop into short lengths. Put in a pan with the herbs and the water. Boil until the leeks are tender. Strain, and retain the stock. Put the leeks in a pie dish. Sprinkle the bacon on top. Beat together the eggs and cream and pour over the leeks. Season with nutmeg, pepper and salt to taste. Pour in ½ pt (285 ml) of the leek stock. Preheat the oven to gas mark 7, 425°F (220°C). Roll out the pastry and cover the pie dish. Seal with a fork, trim, and brush with milk to glaze. Pierce the centre to allow the steam to escape. Bake in the oven until the crust is golden (30–45 minutes).

# Vegetables & Salads

Vegetables have never suffered the same centuries-old prejudice as fresh fruit, partly because so many plants were considered to have medicinal properties. Dishes of raw or cooked vegetables were originally known as 'salads' though this term later came to mean a cold dish. In medieval times, colourful herb and flower salads were eaten in summertime as a welcome change from the boiled roots and cabbage of the winter months. By Elizabeth I's reign, new fruits and vegetables, such as cucumber and lemon, as well as hard-boiled eggs were being added to salads.

In the seventeenth century, onions and shallots continued to be popular, both raw and cooked, but garlic, which had formerly been universally appreciated, began to go out of favour; Elizabethans saw it as the poor man's physic. A century later it was unacceptable in polite circles.

When the nasturtium arrived from America, it was soon taken up as a salad vegetable and the buds were pickled in vinegar to be used like capers. New vegetables have continued to arrive and find a place in English cookery. The potato, originally a native of the Andes, brought about a dramatic change in diet and quickly became popular, unlike the tomato which did not gain acceptance in England until the late eighteenth century.

The caring cook should use only fresh or, if necessary, frozen vegetables. It is now possible to obtain compost-grown and additive-free vegetables from various suppliers and the demand and therefore the supply is inçreasing.

*See also the recipes for:*

Bean Soup

Carrot Soup

Cauliflower Soup

Celery Sauce

Curd and Spinach Tart

Leek Pie

Mushroom Pie

Mushroom Sauce

Onion Pie

Onion Soup

Pea Soup

Pease Pottage

Pickled Cucumber

Pumpkin Pie

Spinach Soup

Spinach with Egg Tart

Tomato Soup

Watercress Soup

## BEETROOT WITH LEEKS

1 lb (450 g) cooked beetroot, sliced

1 lb (450 g) leeks, chopped

2 tablespoons chopped parsley

½ teaspoon powdered cumin

1 tablespoon raisins

freshly ground pepper

salt

1 tablespoon wine vinegar

1 pt (570 ml) vegetable stock

Put the beetroot in a pan with the leeks, parsley, cumin, raisins, pepper and salt to taste. Add the vinegar and stock and simmer together until the leeks are tender.

## BROAD BEAN SALAD

1 lb (450 g) broad beans

salt

2 tablespoons chopped chives

1 tablespoon chopped parsley *or* mint

2 tablespoons olive oil

1 tablespoon wine vinegar

½ teaspoon mustard powder

freshly ground pepper

½ teaspoon salt

1–2 tomatoes, sliced

Boil the beans in slightly salted water until tender. Drain. Put them on a serving dish and sprinkle with chives and parsley. In a bowl, mix together the oil, vinegar, mustard, pepper and salt. Pour them over the beans. Garnish with tomato.

# BROAD BEANS WITH BACON

| | |
|---|---|
| butter *or* cooking oil | 1 teaspoon savory |
| 1 small onion, finely chopped | freshly ground pepper |
| 2 rashers bacon, diced | salt |
| 1 lb (450 g) broad beans | ½ pt (285 ml) stock |
| 1 teaspoon sage | 1 tablespoon chopped parsley |

Heat the butter in a pan and fry the onion until transparent. Add the bacon and fry for 3 minutes. Add the broad beans, sage, savory, pepper and salt to taste. Pour the stock over them and simmer together gently until the beans are tender. Serve garnished with parsley.

# CABBAGE WITH LEEKS

| | |
|---|---|
| 2 tablespoons butter *or* cooking oil | ½ teaspoon caraway seed |
| 1 lb (450 g) leeks, chopped | ½ teaspoon cumin seed |
| 1 lb (450 g) cabbage, chopped | salt |
| freshly ground pepper | ½ pt (285 ml) hot stock *or* water |

Heat the butter in a pan and turn the leeks in it for 2 minutes. Add the cabbage and turn it in the butter. Sprinkle with the spices and salt to taste. Add the hot stock and cook together until the vegetables are just tender.

# BRAISED CELERY

| | |
|---|---|
| 1 head of celery | grated nutmeg |
| butter *or* cooking oil | ½ teaspoon celery seed |
| 1 tablespoon flour | freshly ground pepper |
| 1 cup stock | pinch of salt |
| 1 cup red wine | |

Wash the celery stalks and pat them dry. Cut them in pieces. Heat the butter in a pan and lightly fry the celery for 2 minutes. Stir in the flour. Add the rest of the ingredients. Simmer together for 2 minutes and serve.

# BRAISED CUCUMBER

| | |
|---|---|
| butter *or* cooking oil | 1 blade mace |
| 1 onion, sliced | ½ tablespoon flour |
| 1 cucumber, sliced | chilli powder |
| 1 cup stock | freshly ground pepper |
| 2 tablespoons white wine | salt |

Heat a little butter in a pan and gently fry the onion for 2 minutes. Add the cucumber and fry for 2 more minutes. Add the stock, wine and mace and stew for 5 minutes. Stir in the flour to thicken, and sprinkle with a little chilli powder, pepper and salt to taste. Mix well. Shake the pan as the sauce thickens.

# FRIED HERBS

| | |
|---|---|
| 1 lb (450 g) fresh sorrel *or* spinach, chopped | butter *or* cooking oil |
| 1 bunch parsley, chopped | grated nutmeg |
| 1 bunch spring onions, chopped | freshly ground pepper |
| ½ lettuce, chopped | salt |

Wash the green herbs and onions, trim and shake dry. Heat the butter in a pan and briskly fry the vegetables together for 2 minutes. Sprinkle on the seasoning to taste. Cover the pan, turn down the heat, and allow to cook in the steam for 5 minutes or less.

# HERB SALAD

| | |
|---|---|
| dandelion leaves | curd *or* cottage cheese |
| lettuce | chopped fresh herbs |
| spinach | wine vinegar |
| borage leaves | freshly ground pepper |
| chives | salt |

Chop the green leaves and mix with the cheese and herbs. Sprinkle with a little vinegar, pepper and salt.

## ELIZABETHAN HERB SALAD

For a more elaborate herb salad, try this recipe which was known as compound salad.

In a bowl, mix together the young tips of herbs such as sage, mint, violets, lettuce, chives and spinach. Put in a few shredded blanched almonds, raisins, sliced figs, capers, olives and currants. Sprinkle onto the bowl a little wine vinegar, olive oil, pepper and salt. Mix together and garnish with slices of orange and cucumber.

## EASTER HERB PUDDING

There are many versions of this traditional vegetarian pudding which is eaten during the last two weeks of Lent. Some include barley, oats or breadcrumbs as the filling ingredient. Here is a more delicate pudding using hard-boiled eggs. At Eastertime this pudding is eaten with veal or lamb. In Westmorland, where barley is used as the filler, it is regarded as a 'dainty dish'.

There are many local names for bistort (*Polygonum bistorta*) – Easter ledges, meeks, passion dock – which derive from its use as a basic ingredient in this pudding. The plant is widespread, especially on the damp, hilly pastures of northern England. Use only the arrow-shaped leaves.

| | |
|---|---|
| 1 lb (450 g) young spring leaves (see below) | 1 cup breadcrumbs |
| 2–4 hard-boiled eggs, chopped | 1 cup milk |
| sprig of parsley, chopped | freshly ground pepper |
| | salt |

Take a good bunch of spring leaves, mainly bistort (*Polygonum bistorta*), nettle tops, dandelion leaves, etc. Wash them well and blanch in boiling water for 2 minutes. Strain and chop. In a pudding basin, mix the greens with the eggs, parsley, breadcrumbs, milk, pepper and salt to taste. Cover the bowl with greaseproof paper and steam the pudding by standing it in a pan of boiling water for 30 minutes.

## STEWED LENTILS

1 cup lentils
dripping *or* butter *or*
  cooking oil
1 onion, finely chopped
1 carrot, sliced and chopped
1–3 cloves of garlic,
  finely chopped
2 bay leaves
sprig of fresh mint

1 ham bone (optional)
1 pt (570 ml) water
freshly ground pepper
salt
wine vinegar
1 tablespoon chopped
  parsley

Wash the lentils well and leave to soak in fresh water. Heat the fat in a pan and lightly fry the onion until transparent. Add the carrot and turn it in the fat. Drain the lentils. Add the garlic to the pan with the bay leaves, mint and lentils. Put in the ham bone and 1 pt (570 ml) of water. Season with pepper. Stew together gently for 15 minutes. Check the seasoning for salt. Carry on stewing the lentils until they are soft, adding more liquid if necessary. Stir in a little vinegar, and serve garnished with the parsley.

## MARROW WITH HERB SAUCE

This medieval recipe has hardly changed since it was introduced into England by the Romans.

1 lb (450 g) peeled and cubed
  marrow
salt
2 peppercorns
½ teaspoon cumin seeds
½ teaspoon coriander seeds

a few mint leaves
1 tablespoon ground almonds
1 tablespoon chopped dates
1 teaspoon honey
1 tablespoon olive oil

Put the marrow in a pan with slightly salted water and stew gently until tender. Pour off the liquid and retain. Pound together the peppercorns, cumin, coriander and mint, and then mix them in a bowl with the ground almonds, dates, honey and oil. Put this mixture in a saucepan with a little of the marrow liquid and boil together until it thickens. Pour over the marrow to serve.

# MUSHROOM FRICASSEE

When the moon is in the full,
mushrooms you may freely pull;
But when the moon is on the wane,
wait ere you think to pluck again.

| | |
|---|---|
| 12 oz (340 g) mushrooms | flour |
| salt | 3 tablespoons cream *or* yogurt |
| 1 small onion, finely chopped | grated nutmeg |
| 2–4 cloves | freshly ground pepper |
| small knob of butter | 1 tablespoon chopped parsley |

Put the mushrooms in slightly salted water with the onion and boil for 2 minutes. Add the cloves. Roll the butter in flour and add along with the cream, nutmeg and pepper. Stew together for 5 minutes. Serve garnished with parsley.

# MUSHROOM SALAD

Other herbs such as marjoram or tarragon could be used in this salad, and herb vinegar could replace the cider vinegar (see the recipe for Herb Vinegar).

| | |
|---|---|
| 8 oz (225 g) mushrooms | chopped chives |
| cider vinegar *or* wine vinegar | chopped parsley |

Wash the mushrooms and slice. Sprinkle with the rest of the ingredients and mix together.

# MUSHROOMS IN HONEY

| | |
|---|---|
| 12 oz (340 g) mushrooms | salt |
| butter *or* cooking oil | 1–2 teaspoons honey |
| 1 teaspoon lovage | grated nutmeg |
| freshly ground pepper | |

Wash and slice the mushrooms. Heat the butter in a frying pan and lightly fry the mushrooms. Sprinkle on the lovage, pepper and salt to taste. Mix together and fry for 2 minutes. Add the honey and nutmeg and mix together. Serve immediately.

# DRIED PEAS WITH LEEKS

| | |
|---|---|
| 1 cup dried peas *or* beans | 2 peppercorns |
| 1 lb (450 g) leeks, chopped | ½ teaspoon celery *or* caraway seed |
| 1 tablespoon chopped parsley *or* coriander leaf | fresh basil |
| ½ teaspoon cumin seed | ½ teaspoon salt |
| | wine *or* wine vinegar |

Soak the peas on the morning of the day before you want to make the dish. Drain them and change the water at night. Drain and change the water again next morning. Boil in slightly salted water for 30 minutes, then discard the water. Put in 1 pt (570 ml) of fresh water. Add the leeks and parsley and stew together gently. Meanwhile pound together the cumin, peppercorns, celery seed, basil and salt. Moisten with a little wine or wine vinegar. Add to the peas. Allow to stew until the peas and leeks are tender.

# POTATO SALAD

| | |
|---|---|
| 1½ lb (680 g) potatoes | salt |
| 1 cup yogurt | watercress |
| 2 tablespoons wine vinegar | garlic (optional) |
| 2 tablespoons chopped chives | olive oil *or* melted butter |
| freshly ground pepper | (optional) |

Wash the potatoes and boil in slightly salted water without peeling (peel after cooking if desired). Cut into cubes. In a bowl, mix them with the yogurt, vinegar, chives, pepper and salt to taste. Garnish with watercress.

Finely chopped garlic and olive oil or melted butter may be added to this recipe. Adjust the quantities to suit your taste.

# STEWED RED CABBAGE

2 tablespoons butter *or* cooking oil
1 large onion, chopped
2–4 rashers bacon, chopped
2 cooking apples, peeled, cored and
    sliced
1½ lb (680 g) red cabbage, chopped
2 bay leaves

2 cloves
2–4 peppercorns
1–2 cloves of garlic, finely chopped
salt
1 cup water
2 tablespoons red wine vinegar

Heat the butter in a stew pan and gently fry the onion until transparent. Add the bacon and fry together for 2 minutes. Add the apples, cabbage, herbs and spices. Turn well in the butter. Sprinkle with salt to taste. Add water and vinegar. Cover and cook on low heat until the cabbage is tender.

# SORREL FRICASSEE

This recipe for a much neglected free vegetable can be prepared in a moment. Use only the young leaves.

1½ lb (680 g) sorrel
1–2 tablespoons butter *or*
    cooking oil
1 cup cream *or* yogurt

freshly ground pepper
salt
grated nutmeg

Wash the sorrel and chop. Heat the butter in a pan and turn the sorrel in it for 4 minutes. Add the cream, pepper and salt to taste. Stew together gently, stirring to prevent it burning. Serve sprinkled with nutmeg.

# TURNIPS WITH SWEET AND SOUR SAUCE

This is a medieval way of serving any root vegetable.

1½ lb (680 g) turnips *or* swedes
½ teaspoon cumin seeds
1 teaspoon rue
4 peppercorns
½ teaspoon salt

1–2 teaspoons honey
1–2 tablespoons wine vinegar
1 tablespoon olive oil *or* melted
    butter
1 tablespoon chopped parsley

Peel the turnip and cut in cubes. Boil in slightly salted water until tender. Meanwhile pound together the cumin, rue, peppercorns and salt. Add the honey, vinegar and oil. Mix together with a little of the turnip water. Drain the cooked turnip and toss in sauce. Serve garnished with parsley.

# Eggs & Dairy Produce

In the Middle Ages milk, dairy products and eggs were known collectively as 'white meats'. They were the food of the poor, while fleshmeat and expensive spices characterized the rich person's diet.

Cooked eggs, in their various forms, have suffered from considerable prejudice until recent times. Egg white was considered by the physicians of the early Middle Ages to be bad for the digestion and to produce 'bad blood'. But by the end of the period poached eggs were in vogue. In the late fourteenth century herbolace, a form of scrambled eggs, was popular, as was the tansy, a type of omelette. Boiling eggs in their shells had become common practice by the late sixteenth century and hard-boiled eggs served with butter were the fasting-day food of Tudor times. In *The Court and Kitchin of Elizabeth* (1664), for example, they are served with bitter orange juice, sugar and spices.

Eggs were the symbol of new life and fertility in the countryside and so chicks also feature as an Easter creature. Coloured eggs were the universal Easter gift – often coloured with vegetable dyes and delicately painted.

Today the egg is feared as a contributor to heart disease because the yolk contains cholesterol. The advice that this book gives is the same as for fats. Fats and eggs can both form part of a healthy balanced diet when eaten in moderation and in conjunction with exercise. It is excess in food and diet and lack of exercise that lead to disease.

The Romans took their name for sour milk, *oxygala*, from the Greeks, who probably taught them the practice of using certain herbs to sour and thicken milk. This method was later superseded by the process of using rennet from the stomachs of young animals such as sheep, goats and cows.

When the pastures were opened to cattle on Old May Day, the first day of the Celtic summer, this was the day that cheese-making began.

On Whit Sunday, milkmaids made garlands for the cowherds and enjoyed cold posset and 'white cakes'. On the Monday morning, the first milkmaid to reach a certain pasture was named queen of the pasture for the rest of the summer.

During late summer, butter was salted and potted for the winter – the origin of salted butter, with salt being added as a preservative. Bread and butter with herbs were still a country breakfast in the seventeenth century, and until the Industrial Revolution butter was part of the staple diet of the poor.

*See also the recipes for:*
Syllabub
Yorkshire Curd Tart

## SCRAMBLED EGGS

The herbolace of the early Middle Ages was still being eaten at the end of the fifteenth century, and has hardly changed up to the present day.

| | |
|---|---|
| 6 eggs | 1 tablespoon melted butter |
| small bunch of shredded herbs | 1–2 tablespoons milk |
| freshly ground pepper | ½ cup grated cheese |
| salt | |

Beat the eggs lightly in a bowl. Add the herbs, pepper and salt to taste. Stir in the butter, milk and cheese. Heat a frying pan to medium heat and pour the egg mixture in. Stir with a fork and keep stirring as the mixture cooks. Serve before it is completely set.

# CHEESE AND MUSHROOM OMELETTE

The medieval herbolace and tansy were to be superseded by the omelette, at first referred to in English cookery books as an 'amulet'. In the seventeenth century the omelette could be cooked on one side or turned over and cooked on both sides like a pancake. Eventually the first version became the most popular.

*for each omelette*

| | |
|---|---|
| 1–2 eggs | ½ tablespoon butter *and* ½ |
| pinch of chopped herbs | tablespoon oil, mixed together |
| freshly ground pepper | ½ cup sliced mushrooms |
| salt | ½ cup grated Cheddar cheese |

Beat the eggs lightly in a bowl. Sprinkle in the herbs, pepper and salt to taste. Heat the butter and oil in a frying pan and gently fry the mushrooms for 2 minutes. Pour in the eggs and allow them to run to the edge of the pan. Sprinkle the cheese on top. Serve the omelette, folded in half, as soon as it is set.

# TANSY

In the fourteenth century, the leaves of the tansy (*Chrysanthemum vulgare*) were pounded with other herbs in a mortar. The juice was extracted and added to beaten egg before frying. Early in the seventeenth century this recipe for a simple tansy was reinforced with breadcrumbs, spices and cream. Later it was no longer fried, but boiled in a pudding cloth or baked in a pre-cooked pastry base. The green colour of the dish was then usually made with spinach juice.

This dish can be served with sugar or have candied fruit strewn over it. For a savoury tansy, use salt instead of sugar.

| | |
|---|---|
| 6 eggs | grated nutmeg |
| chopped leaves of tansy | 1 clove, pounded |
| chopped leaves of dandelion | freshly ground pepper |
| *or* other green herb | salt |
| 2–4 tablespoons breadcrumbs | 1 tablespoon butter |
| 1–2 tablespoons cream *or* | |
| yogurt | |

Beat the eggs lightly in a bowl and add the herbs, breadcrumbs, cream, spices and salt to taste. Heat the butter gently in a frying pan. Add the egg mixture and cook until set.

## YORKSHIRE PUDDING

When wheat flour had come into common use for cakes and puddings, economically minded cooks in the North of England found a way of using the fat which fell into the dripping pan to make a batter pudding which could cook while the meat roasted. In *The Whole Duty of a Woman* (1737), the recipe appeared as 'A dripping pudding'. Ten years later, Hannah Glasse was calling it 'Yorkshire Pudding' in her own cookery book.

Try adding currants to the batter when used with beef. Add a little chopped sage leaf and chives or onion when eaten with pork. Serve plain with lamb. Yorkshire pudding is a delicious dessert if you serve it with a dressing of melted butter and treacle. On special occasions, add cream or yogurt.

| | |
|---|---|
| 3 oz (85 g) flour | freshly ground pepper |
| 1 egg | salt |
| 3 fl oz (85 ml) milk | 2 tablespoons dripping |
| 2 fl oz (55 ml) water | *or* cooking oil |

Preheat the oven to gas mark 7, 425°F (220°C). Sift the flour into a bowl. Make a well in the middle and break in the egg. Gradually beat in the milk, water and seasoning to taste. Put the fat in the baking tin and place it in the oven. When the fat is smoking hot, pour in the batter and bake in the oven until the pudding has risen and is crisp and golden (25–30 minutes). Have the roast beef 'resting' in the meantime. Serve the pudding straight away since it will begin to go soggy.

Traditionally, Yorkshire pudding was served before the meat with gravy poured over it. This filled you up nicely so you did not need so much meat afterwards. It is of course an excellent accompaniment to roast meat, served with a sauce, vegetables and gravy.

## ELDERFLOWER PANCAKES

Pancake batter was made with flour, eggs, powdered spices and either milk or water. Pancakes became especially popular as a pre-Lenten dish because they were a handy way of using up fat, flour and eggs. Today this tradition survives as Pancake Day, and for many people Shrove Tuesday is the only day on which they ever prepare pancakes. The traditional Olney Pancake Race is thought to have been run since 1450.

| | |
|---|---|
| 4 sprigs of elderflower | 10 fl oz (285 ml) pancake liquid |
| 4 oz (110 g) flour | made of 7 fl oz (200 ml) milk |
| pinch of salt | and 3 fl oz (85 ml) water |
| 1 egg | butter |
| | 1 lemon, sliced |

Break up the elderflower sprigs. Sift the flour and salt together in a mixing bowl. Make a well in the centre and break in the egg. Gradually beat in half the liquid so that the flour is completely mixed with the egg and liquid. Beat in the rest of the liquid with the elderflowers. Allow the mixture to stand for 30 minutes. Fry large spoonfuls of batter in hot butter until golden on both sides. Serve with slices of lemon.

## PINK PANCAKES

Gervase Markham, in *The English Hus-wife* (1615), considered that pancakes made with new milk or cream were 'tough and cloying, not crisp and pleasant' as running water would have made them. By the late eighteenth century, however, these were the ingredients that were generally used. Other vegetables and flavourings may be used to make variations on this eighteenth-century pancake.

| | |
|---|---|
| 1 cooked beetroot | freshly grated nutmeg |
| 4 oz (110 g) flour | 1–2 tablespoons brandy *or* |
| pinch of salt | sherry |
| 2 eggs | butter |
| 3 tablespoons single cream | preserved angelica |
| 1 teaspoon sugar | preserved fruit |

Skin the beetroot and reduce to a thin puree. Sift the flour and salt together in a mixing bowl. Make a well in the centre and break in the eggs. Make a pancake liquid by mixing 7 tablespoons of beetroot puree with the cream. Gradually beat half of this liquid into the flour so that it is completely mixed with the eggs and liquid. Beat in the rest of the liquid with the sugar, nutmeg and brandy. Beat together and allow to stand for 30 minutes. Fry large spoonfuls of the batter in a little hot butter until golden on both sides. Serve garnished with preserved angelica and preserved fruit.

# SAVOURY PANCAKES

A stuffed pancake may be made by frying the batter first and then filling
with a stuffing mixture of fish etc. and herbs.

| | |
|---|---|
| 4 oz (110 g) flour | 1 teaspoon herbs |
| pinch of salt | freshly ground pepper |
| 1 egg | salt |
| ½ pt (285 ml) water | dripping *or* butter *or* cooking |
| 8 oz (225 g) cooked cod, | oil |
| cooked minced meat *or* | 1 lemon, sliced |
| cooked mashed vegetables | |

Make the batter by sifting the flour with the salt in a mixing bowl. Make a
well in the centre and break in the egg. Gradually beat in half of the water
so that the flour is completely mixed with the egg and water. Beat in the
rest of the water. Add the savoury ingredients, herbs, pepper and salt to
taste. Fry large spoonfuls of batter in hot fat until golden on both sides.
Serve with slices of lemon.

# EGG TART WITH HERBS

The secret of a good egg tart is to bake the pastry case in a flan tin before the
filling is cooked in it. The old method of baking 'blind' was to put a piece of
greaseproof paper on the pastry with some rice or bread crusts on it. It was
then baked in a moderate oven for 15 minutes. The hot pastry case was
then filled, and baked again. The method given below is a little less
complicated, but effective. Any mixture of herbs may be used in this
traditional egg tart, as well as mushrooms, nuts and cheese.

*for the pastry*

| | |
|---|---|
| 4 oz (110 g) flour | 1 oz (30 g) butter |
| pinch of salt | cold water |
| 1 oz (30 g) lard | |

*for the filling*

| | |
|---|---|
| 1 tablespoon dripping *or* butter *or* cooking oil | 2 tablespoons chopped fresh herbs |
| 1 small onion, finely chopped, *or* 2 spring onions, chopped | 2–3 eggs |
| 2 tablespoons chopped parsley | ½ pt (285 ml) cream |
| 2 tablespoons chopped dandelion *or* spinach leaf | freshly grated nutmeg |
| | freshly ground pepper |
| | salt |

First, make up the shortcrust pastry. Sift the flour with the salt. Rub in the lard and butter to make 'crumbs'. Add enough water to make a soft, springy dough. Wrap in polythene and keep in a cool place for 20 minutes to allow the gluten time to react with the water. After 10 minutes, preheat the oven to gas mark 4, 350°F (180°C), and put a baking sheet on the centre shelf. Roll out the pastry large enough to fit a greased flan tin with enough for the sides. Press into position and prick all over with a fork. Bake for 15 minutes on the baking sheet. Remove from the oven and brush all over with beaten egg. Return it to the oven and bake for a further 5 minutes.

While the pastry case is baking, make the filling. Heat the fat gently in a pan and fry the onion until transparent. Add the herbs and turn in the fat for 1 minute. Remove from the heat. In a bowl beat the eggs with the cream. Season with nutmeg, pepper and salt to taste. Stir in the onion and herbs. Pour into the hot flan case and bake in the oven until the centre of the filling is set and the tart pastry is golden (30–40 minutes).

## SPINACH AND EGG TART

*for the pastry*

| 6 oz (170 g) flour | pinch of salt |
| 1 teaspoon baking powder | 3 oz (85 g) butter or lard |

*for the filling*

| 1 lb (450 g) spinach, chopped | freshly ground pepper |
| 2 eggs | 2 oz (60 g) grated Cheddar cheese |
| 1 pinch each of pennyroyal, thyme, savory | |

Make the egg tart in the same way as in the previous recipe. Make up the shortcrust pastry, allow to rest, then bake the pastry case at gas mark 4, 350°F (180°C). Mix the spinach and eggs in a bowl with the herbs, pepper and cheese. Fill the pastry case and bake in the oven for a further 40–45 minutes.

# SPICY CHEESE TART

| | |
|---|---|
| 4 oz (110 g) flour | 1 cup breadcrumbs |
| pinch of salt | ½ teaspoon powdered ginger |
| 1 oz (30 g) butter | ½ teaspoon powdered cinnamon |
| 1 oz (30 g) lard | 1 tablespoon sugar |
| 1½–2 tablespoons cold water | grated nutmeg |
| 8 oz (225 g) curd cheese | chopped mixed peel |
| 4 egg yolks | |

Sift the flour into a mixing bowl. Cut the cold butter and lard into the flour with a knife. Rub the pieces of fat into the flour until you have a crumbly consistency. Do not let the flour get warm. Add cold water gradually, stirring in with the knife. Knead together to make a smooth dough which does not stick to your hands. Wrap the dough in polythene and keep in a cool place until required. In a bowl mix together the curd cheese, egg yolks, breadcrumbs, ginger, cinnamon and sugar. Preheat the oven to gas mark 7, 425°F (220°C). Roll out the pastry to fit an 8 in (20 cm) tart tin. Grease the tin and lay the pastry in it. Put in the filling and smooth over with a spoon. Sprinkle with nutmeg and bake in the oven until the pastry and the cheese mixture are golden brown. Sprinkle over some mixed peel while the tart is still warm and allow to cool before cutting. On special occasions serve with cream.

# CHEESE POTTAGE

It was common in the seventeenth century for pottages to be strengthened with cheese. The basis could be any kind of meat, fish, poultry or game as well as a vegetable pottage.

| | |
|---|---|
| ½ cup lentils | 1–2 cloves, pounded |
| 1½ pt (850 ml) water | grated nutmeg |
| 1–2 bay leaves | pinch of powdered mace |
| freshly ground pepper | breadcrumbs or ground almonds |
| salt | (optional) |
| 1 cup grated Cheddar | |
| cheese | |

Wash the lentils and put in a soup pan with the water. Add the bay leaves, pepper and salt to taste. Simmer gently until the lentils begin to soften. Add the cheese, cloves, nutmeg and mace. Stew until the pottage thickens. Breadcrumbs or ground almonds can be added to give extra body to the pottage.

## SPICY CURD CHEESE

This Elizabethan recipe makes a tasty, nourishing sweet dish.

| | |
|---|---|
| 8 oz (225 g) curd cheese | 1 tablespoon rosewater |
| ½ teaspoon powdered cinnamon | 1–2 teaspoons sugar |
| grated nutmeg | |

Mix the ingredients together. For a special treat, serve with cream.

## CURD AND SPINACH TART

This recipe is adapted from one in *The English Art of Cookery* (1788).

| | |
|---|---|
| 4 oz (110 g) spinach | 1 teaspoon sugar |
| 8 oz (225 g) curd cheese | grated nutmeg |
| 4 oz (110 g) ground almonds | 8 oz (225 g) puff pastry |
| 4 oz (110 g) currants | |

Boil the spinach for 5 minutes in slightly salted water and chop finely. Preheat the oven to gas mark 7, 425°F (220°C). In a bowl mix the curd with the almonds, currants, spinach, sugar and nutmeg. Line an 8–10 in (20–25 cm) tart tin with three-quarters of the pastry. Fill with the cheese mixture. Roll out the rest of the pastry and cut in thin strips. Lay across the top of the tart to make a lattice effect. Sprinkle with more sugar if desired. Bake in the oven until the pastry is golden (20–30 minutes).

## CURD FRITTERS

| | |
|---|---|
| 4 oz (110 g) flour | 1 egg |
| pinch of salt | ½ pt (285 ml) yogurt |
| 1 clove, pounded | oil for deep frying |
| pinch of powdered mace | oranges |
| grated nutmeg | |

Sift the flour with the salt and spices. Make a well in the centre and break in the egg. Gradually stir in the yogurt until everything is well mixed. Leave the batter to 'rest' for 30 minutes. Drop spoonsful of batter into hot oil and deep fry until golden. Drain on kitchen paper. Serve with segments of orange.

# HERB AND SPICE BUTTERS

Combinations of herbs and butter, to be eaten with wholewheat bread, had been recommended by Tudor physicians: from the early sixteenth century the extracted oils of sage as well as those of cinnamon, nutmeg and mace were being mixed with butter. Recipes in *The Family Dictionary* (1696) describe how to make a range of herb butters in this way. Small amounts of fresh herbs can be finely chopped and mixed with butter to produce a similar result. They may be potted and will keep for a few days in a cool place. Herb or spice butters may be made up according to your own requirements and there is plenty of scope for your own experiments.

### PARSLEY BUTTER

| | |
|---|---|
| 2 oz (60 g) butter | salt |
| 2 teaspoons finely chopped parsley | freshly ground pepper |

Mix the butter with the parsley and season with a pinch of salt and pepper. Serve with fish or meat or as a spread on bread or toast.

### MIXED HERB BUTTER

| | |
|---|---|
| 1 tablespoon chopped chives | 1 tablespoon chervil *or* borage |
| 1 tablespoon spinach *or* dandelion leaf | 2 oz (60 g) butter |
| 1 tablespoon parsley | salt |
| | freshly ground pepper |

Blanch the herbs in hot water. Drain well and chop finely. Mix well with the butter. Season to taste.

### CAPER BUTTER

| | |
|---|---|
| 2 oz (60 g) butter | salt |
| 2–3 tablespoons finely chopped capers *or* nasturtium buds | freshly ground pepper |

Mix the butter with the herbs. Season to taste. Serve with fish dishes.

### HERB AND NUT BUTTER

| | |
|---|---|
| 2 tablespoons hazelnuts | 2 oz (60 g) butter |
| chopped herbs e.g. parsley, chives, sage | salt |
| | freshly ground pepper |

Pound the hazelnuts with the herbs. Mix well with the butter. Season if necessary.

## RUM OR BRANDY BUTTER

Rum is the preferred ingredient in Cumberland, while brandy is substituted in other parts of the country.

| | |
|---|---|
| **8 oz (225 g) butter** | **pinch of cinnamon** |
| **12 oz (340 g) sugar** | **1 glass rum** *or* **brandy** |
| **freshly grated nutmeg** | |

Put the butter in a bowl in a warm place to soften. Beat in the sugar, nutmeg and cinnamon. Gradually beat in the rum and allow the butter to set. Serve with Christmas pudding.

# Sauces, Gravies & Stuffings

The essence of the good medieval pottage was the sauce, and such was their excellence that these sauces came to be served separately with meat or fish. For roast meat or boiled fish, sauces were often served in small bowls placed near the trencher plates of the diners. The liquid base was usually vinegar, but it could also be wine, ale or milk. The cooks of the wealthy needed to be skilled in judging the right quantities for saucemaking. Such skilled cooks were much in demand and they could hire themselves out as professional saucemakers.

The seventeenth century saw sauces becoming thinner and by the end of the eighteenth century intricate sauces were disappearing. Most households simply made a gravy from dripping and water, thickened with flour.

*See also the recipes for:*

Baked Fish with Mustard Sauce
Baked Ham with Green Stuffing
Caper Butter
Haddock Soup with Forcemeat Balls
Haddock with Forcemeat Balls
Herb and Nut Butter

Herrings with Mustard Sauce
Mixed Herb Butter
Mussels in Herb Sauce
Oysters in Lovage Sauce
Parsley Butter
Pork Chops with Juniper Sauce

Rabbit with Forcemeat Balls
Roast Chicken with Chestnut Stuffing
Roast Chicken with Date Stuffing
Roast Duck with Damson Sauce
Roast Goose with Fruit Sauce
Roast Turkey with Mushroom Sauce
Rum or Brandy Butter
Stewed Steak with Mushrooms and Wine Sauce
Stuffed Heart

## APPLE SAUCE

| | |
|---|---|
| cooking apples, peeled, cored and sliced | cinnamon butter |
| lemon peel | sugar |
| cloves | |

Put the apples in a little water in a saucepan with some pieces of lemon peel, cloves and cinnamon. Cook gently until the apple is soft. Remove the lemon peel and spices and mash the apple with a little butter and sugar. Serve with pork.

## BREAD SAUCE

To make a currant sauce for pork, follow this recipe and boil some currants with the bread.

| | |
|---|---|
| stale bread | 1 blade of mace |
| ½ pt (285 ml) water | peppercorns |
| 1 onion stuck with 4 cloves | butter salt |

Put chunks of stale bread in the water with the clove onion, mace and a few peppercorns in a cloth. Boil for a few minutes. Take out the onion and spices. Mash the bread and add a piece of butter and a pinch of salt.

# CELERY SAUCE

| | |
|---|---|
| 4–6 sticks celery, chopped | salt |
| 1 pt (570 ml) stock *or* water | 1 tablespoon butter |
| freshly ground pepper | 1 tablespoon flour |
| grated nutmeg | 2 tablespoons cream *or* yogurt |
| ½ teaspoon celery seeds (optional) | |

Put the celery in a pan with the stock, spices and salt to taste. Stew gently until the celery is tender. Liquidize the celery or rub it through a coarse sieve. In a frying pan heat the butter, stir in the flour and allow to brown gently. Add a little of the celery stock and mix. Pour the pan contents into the stock. Stir in the cream and heat together gently until the sauce thickens.

Serve with ham or poultry. For a more emphatic celery taste, add ½ teaspoon of celery seeds to the spices.

# CIDER SAUCE

| | |
|---|---|
| 1 pt (570 ml) cider | 2 cloves |
| ¾ pt (425 ml) thick | freshly ground pepper |
|    brown stock | salt |
| 1 bay leaf | |

Mix all the ingredients together and simmer in a pan until reduced to two-thirds of the original quantity. Serve with ham or pork.

The sauce can also be used as a marinade for meat or as a stewing liquid.

# EGG SAUCE

| | |
|---|---|
| 2 eggs, hard-boiled | 1 tablespoon butter |
| 1 pt (570 ml) milk | 1 tablespoon flour |
| 1 bay leaf | freshly ground pepper |
| 1 tablespoon finely chopped | grated nutmeg |
|    parsley | salt |

Chop the eggs finely. Put the milk in a pan with the bay leaf and parsley. Heat together gently for 3 minutes. In a frying pan melt the butter and lightly brown the flour. Add a little of the milk and stir together. Pour into the rest of the milk. Add the eggs, pepper, nutmeg and salt to taste. Heat together gently until the sauce thickens.

Serve with fish, or a vegetable such as cauliflower or onions.

# FISH SAUCE

| | |
|---|---|
| ½ pt (285 ml) cooked fish stock | 1 glass white wine |
| 1–2 tablespoons finely chopped | 1 tablespoon flour |
|   chives *or* spring onion | 1 tablespoon cream *or* yogurt |
| 1 anchovy, chopped | |

Mix the fish stock in a saucepan with the chives, anchovy and wine. Mix the flour with ½ cup of this liquid and stir in. Add the cream. Simmer together gently until the sauce thickens.

Shellfish such as oysters, cockles or prawns could be added to this sauce. Red wine may be used as long as the cream is omitted.

# GOOSEBERRY SAUCE

| | |
|---|---|
| stewed gooseberries | melted butter *or* cream |
| powdered ginger |   *or* yogurt |

Combine the gooseberries with a little powdered ginger and butter. Serve with pork, goose and game.

# GREEN SAUCE

Writing in the twelfth century, Alexander Neckham listed sage, parsley, costmary, dittany and thyme as ingredients. Such a sauce became very popular when served with fish. By the late eighteenth century, however, it was rarely used, having been replaced by preserved pickles, ketchup and bottled sauces.

| | |
|---|---|
| green herbs | breadcrumbs |
| cloves of garlic | wine *or* wine vinegar *or* |
| peppercorns |   ale |
| salt | |

Grind together any available green herbs with the garlic and peppercorns to taste. Add a little salt. Thicken with breadcrumbs which have been moistened with a little wine.

# HERB SAUCE

The green sauce of the previous recipe lived on under other guises such as this one, which appeared in *The Illustrated London Cookery Book* of 1852.

| | |
|---|---|
| 1 tablespoon butter | chopped herbs (see below) |
| 1 tablespoon flour | ½ pt (285 ml) stock |

Melt the butter in a pan and gently brown the flour in it. Put in some chopped herbs such as parsley, tarragon, borage, chervil, cress and spring onion. Add the stock and boil together gently for 15 minutes. Serve hot.

# HORSERADISH SAUCE

The horseradish root is extremely hot and the fumes from a grated root will irritate your eyes, but this home-made sauce will repay your perseverance.

| | |
|---|---|
| 2 tablespoons grated horseradish root | 2 teaspoons wine vinegar |
| 1 teaspoon sugar | 5 fl oz (140 ml) cream *or* yogurt, beaten smooth |
| ½ teaspoon mustard powder | freshly ground pepper |
| 2 teaspoons lemon juice | pinch of salt |

Mix all the ingredients together. Keep in a cool place. Serve with roast beef, fish or cold tongue.

# MUSHROOM SAUCE

| | |
|---|---|
| 1 tablespoon butter | pinch of salt |
| 4 oz (110 g) mushrooms, sliced | 1 pt (570 ml) cream *or* yogurt |
| ½–1 teaspoon powdered mace | 2 egg yolks |

Heat the butter gently in a saucepan and fry the mushrooms with the mace and salt for 2 minutes. Add the cream and egg yolks and stir together well. Keep stirring until the mixture begins to thicken. Serve with poultry and slices of lemon.

## POULTRY SAUCE

| | |
|---|---|
| chicken giblets and bones | ½ teaspoon salt |
| 1 pt (570 ml) water | 2 tablespoons cream *or* yogurt |
| small bunch of sweet herbs | 1 tablespoon butter |
| 2 spring onions, chopped | 1 cup sliced mushrooms |
| 1 slice lemon peel | ½ teaspoon powdered mace |
| 4–6 peppercorns | 1 tablespoon flour |

Put the giblets and bones in a pan with the water. Add the herbs, onion, lemon peel, peppercorns and salt and boil together gently for 20 minutes. Strain off ½ pt (285 ml) of stock and stir in the cream. In a frying pan heat the butter and fry the mushrooms for 2 minutes. Sprinkle with the mace. Add the flour and mix together. Add to the sauce and cook together until it thickens. Serve with poultry and slices of lemon.

## SAUCE FOR ROAST LAMB OR MUTTON

This recipe appears in *The Accomplisht Cook* (1665), where it also includes the juice from fresh oysters.

| | |
|---|---|
| 2 tablespoons dripping *or* butter *or* cooking oil | 1 glass claret |
| 1 small onion, finely chopped | ½ pt (285 ml) stock *or* roasting juices |
| 2 tablespoons capers *or* nasturtium buds | grated nutmeg |
| | ½ teaspoon salt |

Heat the fat in a saucepan and gently fry the onion until golden. Add the rest of the ingredients and stew together.

## VENISON SAUCE

| | |
|---|---|
| ½ pt (285 ml) stock | 1 tablespoon currants |
| 1 glass port *or* red wine | freshly ground pepper |
| 4 cloves | ½ teaspoon salt |
| 1 cup breadcrumbs | |

Boil the ingredients together gently until the sauce thickens. Serve hot with venison or venison pie.

## FAMILY CULLIS

A cullis is a thick gravy. This cullis is suggested by Jennings in *Two Thousand Five Hundred Practical Recipes in Family Cookery* (1844). Traditionally the cullis would be strained before use.

| | |
|---|---|
| 2 tablespoons dripping *or* butter | 1 bay leaf |
| 1 tablespoon flour | ½ teaspoon basil |
| ½ pt (285 ml) stock | 2 cloves |
| 1 glass white wine | freshly grated nutmeg |
| 1 tablespoon finely chopped parsley | freshly ground pepper |
| ½ teaspoon thyme | ½ teaspoon salt |
| | sliced mushrooms (optional) |

Heat the fat in a pan and gently brown the flour. Add the rest of the ingredients. Stew together gently until the cullis thickens.

## GRAVY FOR FOWL

Gravies can be served quite thin, but they should not, like many sauces, include any milk, cream or yogurt.

| | |
|---|---|
| giblets | freshly ground pepper |
| ½ pt (285 ml) water | salt |
| ½ teaspoon thyme | 1 glass red wine |

Boil the giblets with the water, herbs and seasonings until the giblets are tender, adding more water if necessary. Pour off the stock into another pan. Add the wine. Pound the cooked liver and add to the gravy. Thicken with flour if necessary.

## HERB GRAVY

Here is a gem from *The Lady's Assistant* of 1759 – a gravy made totally with vegetables.

| | |
|---|---|
| any vegetables available | freshly ground pepper |
| fresh herbs | salt |

Simply boil up a number of vegetables with plenty of water until they are soft. Liquidize them or rub through a coarse sieve and add herbs and seasoning to taste. Boil together gently for 15 minutes.

# BREAD AND BACON STUFFING

Another way to add interest to meat and fish was to stuff them with what became known as forcemeat. Like sauces, the creation of good forcemeats became one of the great culinary arts. Some of the seventeenth-century forcemeats were quite exotic, including breadcrumbs, minced meat, herbs, spices, and dried and crystallized fruits. To create extra interest, they may be coloured yellow with saffron or green with spinach juice. A century later, the plentiful supply of cheap oysters made them a favourite stuffing ingredient to take the place of the sweet fruits.

As well as being used to fill the cavity of a bird or joint of meat, stuffings may be cooked separately, either in a dish or made up into forcemeat balls. Cook stuffings in a covered dish for about 45 minutes at gas mark 4, 350°F (180°C), or for 30 minutes if made into balls. Forcemeat balls may also be gently fried until golden.

| | |
|---|---|
| 6 oz (170 g) breadcrumbs | 2 tablespoons chopped fresh herbs |
| milk | grated nutmeg |
| 4 oz (110 g) bacon, minced *or* finely chopped | freshly ground pepper |
| | ½ teaspoon salt |
| 2 teaspoons grated lemon peel | 1 egg, beaten |

In a bowl, moisten the breadcrumbs with a little warm milk. Add the rest of the ingredients and mix together well. Use as a stuffing or to make forcemeat balls to serve with roast meat.

## SAUSAGE AND PRUNE STUFFING

| | |
|---|---|
| 6 oz (170 g) prunes *or* dried apricots | ½ teaspoon powdered ginger *or* 1 teaspoon finely chopped fresh ginger |
| 8 oz (225 g) sausagemeat | grated nutmeg |
| 1 tablespoon finely chopped parsley | freshly ground pepper |
| ½ teaspoon powdered cinnamon | ½ teaspoon salt |
| | 1 egg, beaten |

Soak the prunes overnight in water. Next day simmer them until soft. Drain, and retain the liquid for making gravy. Remove the stones. In a bowl mix the prunes with the rest of the ingredients. Beat well together. This is an excellent stuffing for goose.

## STUFFING FOR TURKEY

6 oz (170 g) breadcrumbs
milk
2 oz (60 g) raisins
2 oz (60 g) almonds, blanched and
  shredded
2 oz (60 g) butter
2 teaspoons grated lemon peel

a few sprigs of parsley, chopped
small bunch of sweet herbs
1 tablespoon cream *or* yogurt
1 egg, beaten
grated nutmeg
freshly ground pepper
½ teaspoon salt

In a bowl, moisten the breadcrumbs with a little warm milk. Add the rest
of the ingredients and mix well together.

## STUFFING FOR FOWL

4 oz (110 g) breadcrumbs
milk
6 oz (170 g) sausagemeat
2 oz (60 g) butter
2 oz (60 g) mushrooms, chopped
2 teaspoons grated lemon peel

small bunch of sweet herbs
½ teaspoon powdered mace
2 tablespoons finely chopped parsley
1 egg, beaten
freshly ground pepper
½ teaspoon salt

In a bowl, moisten the breadcrumbs with a little warm milk. Add the rest
of the ingredients and mix well together.

# Puddings

During his travels in England, the French writer Misson discovered the wonders of pudding. Later, in his *Memoirs* (1719), he exclaimed 'Blessed be he that invented pudding!'

*See also the recipes for:*
Curd Fritters
Elderflower Pancakes
Pink Pancakes
Spicy Cheese Tart
Spicy Curd Cheese
Tansy
Yorkshire Curd Tart
Yorkshire Pudding

## BREAD AND BUTTER PUDDING

| | |
|---|---|
| 1 pt (570 ml) milk | 3 eggs |
| 3 tablespoons sugar | butter |
| 1 bay leaf | bread |
| 2 teaspoons grated lemon peel | currants *or* raisins *or* sultanas |
| small stick cinnamon | |

Put the milk in a pan with the sugar, bay leaf, lemon peel and cinnamon and simmer gently for 15 minutes. Leave to cool. Strain. Preheat the oven to gas mark 4, 350°F (180°C). Beat the eggs well and add to the milk. Smear a pie dish with butter. Put in a layer of bread and butter, then sprinkle with a layer of currants. Put in more layers until the dish is almost full. Pour the milk and egg mixture over the top. Bake in the oven until the top is golden (about 45 minutes).

Nuts and other fruits may be added to this simple pudding. Serve with cream or yogurt on special occasions.

## SIMPLE PLUM PUDDING

Sing, sing,
What shall I sing?
The cat's run away
With the pudding string!
Do, do,
What shall I do?
The cat's run away
With the pudding too!

| | |
|---|---|
| 6 oz (170 g) flour | 1 teaspoon mixed spice *or* 3 allspice |
| ½ teaspoon bicarbonate of soda | berries, pounded |
| 6 oz (170 g) shredded suet | 2 tablespoons sugar |
| 6 oz (170 g) breadcrumbs | ½ cup golden syrup *or* treacle |
| 6 oz (170 g) raisins *or* sultanas | ½ cup milk |
| 6 oz (170 g) currants | ½ cup stout |
| 6 oz (170 g) mixed peel | butter |

Sift the flour with the bicarbonate of soda in a bowl. Stir in the suet. Add the breadcrumbs, raisins, currants, peel, spice and sugar. In a separate bowl mix the treacle, milk and stout. (The best way to weigh out treacle and syrup is to weigh the tin or pot on the scales, then spoon out the required amount straight to where it is required.) Pour this into the flour and fruit mixture and stir well together. Grease a pudding basin with butter and fill with the pudding mixture. Cover with a round of buttered greaseproof paper or foil and steam for 4 hours.

# FIGGY PUDDING

Originally 'figgey' was a medieval meatless pottage made for Lent. During the Middle Ages, people found no need to separate the tastes of sweet and savoury.

| | |
|---|---|
| 5 oz (140 g) flour | grated nutmeg |
| 2½ oz (70 g) shredded suet | 3 oz (85 g) treacle *or* golden |
| 4 oz (110 g) figs, chopped, *or* stoned | syrup |
| dates, chopped | 1 egg, beaten |
| ½ teaspoon powdered cinnamon | 3 oz (85 g) yogurt *or* sour milk *or* |
| ½ teaspoon powdered ginger | buttermilk |
| ½ teaspoon bicarbonate of soda | butter |

Mix the dry ingredients together in a bowl. Heat the treacle gently in a saucepan. Mix in the egg and yogurt. Pour into the dry ingredients and mix together well. Grease a pudding basin and pour in the pudding mixture. Leave at least 1 in (3 cm) spare at the top to allow for the pudding to expand. Cut a round of greaseproof paper, smear it with butter and put the buttered side on top of the pudding. Steam for 2 hours. Serve hot with cream, yogurt or custard.

# UPSIDE DOWN GINGER PUDDING

| | |
|---|---|
| ½ tablespoon sugar | 5 fl oz (140 ml) milk |
| 3 Conference pears | 1 teaspoon bicarbonate of soda |
| 4 oz (110 g) butter | 8 oz (225 g) flour |
| 4 oz (110 g) golden syrup | 1 teaspoon powdered cinnamon |
| 4 oz (110 g) black treacle | 1 teaspoon powdered ginger |
| 1 egg | |

Preheat the oven to gas mark 4, 350°F (180°C). Line the base and sides of an 8 in (20 cm) cake tin with greaseproof paper which has been smeared with butter. Sprinkle the base with the sugar. Peel, halve and core the pears. Place them, cut side down, on the sugar. Put the butter, syrup and treacle in a pan and melt together over a low heat. Remove from the heat. In a bowl, beat the egg with the milk and bicarbonate of soda. Stir into the treacle mixture. Sift the flour with the cinnamon and ginger. Make a well in the centre and pour the treacle mixture into it. Stir the flour into the liquid until the whole is well blended together. Pour into the prepared cake tin. Bake in the oven until the pudding has risen and is firm to the touch (about 1½ hours). Turn onto a plate so that the pears are now uppermost. Remove the lining paper.

The pudding can be eaten hot with cream or custard, or served cold.

## CLIPPING PUDDING

> Wife, make us a dinner, spare fleshe neither corn,
> Make wafers and cakes for our sheepe must be shorne.
>
> Elizabethan verse

Hard-working days of sheep-shearing in the summer months were followed by hearty meals and shearing dances with the womenfolk in the evenings. At dinnertime, the shearers washed their hands in pails of water laced with sprigs of wild mint, which was found to be effective for removing both the grease and the smell of the fleece. Gingerbread was a favourite afternoon snack of sheep-shearers, with a clipping pudding at the end of the day.

| | |
|---|---|
| 8 oz (225 g) short grain rice | 4 oz (110 g) currants |
| 1 pt (570 ml) milk | 4 oz (110 g) raisins *or* sultanas |
| ½ teaspoon powdered cinnamon | 1 tablespoon butter |
| 3 tablespoons sugar | grated nutmeg |
| 1 egg, beaten | |

Wash the rice in cold water. Put it in a pan with the milk, cinnamon and sugar and simmer gently until the rice is tender. Preheat the oven to gas mark 4, 350°F (180°C). Stir in the egg, dried fruit and butter. Pour into an ovenproof dish and sprinkle with nutmeg. Bake in the oven until a nice brown skin has formed on the top of the pudding (about 20 minutes).

## CHRISTMAS PUDDING

Holly is a male emblem which was thought to bring fortune and fertility to the household. Ivy, of clinging habit, is the female symbol. Apart from Yuletide, for the rest of the year there was a ritual taboo against touching holly. The earliest day when holly or mistletoe could safely enter the house (and then only with a man) was Christmas Eve. Holly was kept and burned under the following year's Christmas pudding as a charm of continuity.

Flour of England, fruit of Spain,
Met together in a shower of rain;
Put in a bag, tied round with string;
If you tell me this riddle,
I'll give you a ring.

Christmas pudding is a more elaborate version of the steamed plum pudding, specifically for Christmas, which has hardly changed for centuries. It should be made a month or two before it is needed, and, traditionally, stirred by every member of the family. Each has three wishes, one of which will be granted. The puddings are then set aside to await the return of absent people.

A mixture of butter and lard may be substituted for the suet.

| | |
|---|---|
| 3 oz (85 g) flour | 1 tablespoon black treacle *or* |
| ½ teaspoon baking powder | golden syrup |
| pinch of salt | 4 oz (110 g) chopped mixed peel |
| 1 teaspoon ground mixed spice | grated peel of ½ lemon |
| grated nutmeg | grated peel of ½ orange |
| 8 oz (225 g) raisins | 1 tablespoon grated carrot |
| 8 oz (225 g) currants | 3 eggs, beaten |
| 8 oz (225 g) sultanas | 6 tablespoons stout |
| 5 oz (140 g) breadcrumbs | 3 tablespoons brandy *or* sherry |
| 6 oz (170 g) sugar | butter |
| 8 oz (225 g) shredded suet | |

Sift the flour with the baking powder, salt and spices in a large bowl. Add the fruit, breadcrumbs, sugar and suet. In a separate bowl mix the treacle with the citrus peel and carrot. Stir in the eggs and stout and beat together. Add this to the flour and fruit mixture and mix well. Cover and leave overnight in a cool place. Next day stir in the brandy. Grease two pudding basins and fill them with the pudding mixture. Cover with rounds of greaseproof paper which have also been smeared with butter. Cover each basin with a cloth, tie round the rim of the basin with string and then tie the ends of the cloth together over the top so that the basins can be lifted by the knotted 'handle'. Steam for 6 hours. Remove the coverings and allow to cool. Store in a cool, dry place.

When needed, steam again for 2 hours. Serve by upending onto a dish. Just before serving, make a small depression in the top of the upended pudding and fill with brandy or rum, pouring some over the sides. Set fire to the brandy, switch off the lights and bring to the table. Happy Christmas!

# SPECIAL RICE PUDDING

This seventeenth-century recipe is said to have been relished by King William of Orange.

| | |
|---|---|
| 2 oz (60 g) short grain rice | 4 oz (110 g) sugar |
| ¾ pt (425 ml) milk | ½ teaspoon powdered cinnamon |
| 2 oz (60 g) butter | 3 tablespoons cream *or* yogurt |
| 12 oz (340 g) puff pastry | grated nutmeg |
| 4 eggs | |

Wash the rice in cold water, drain and simmer in the milk until tender. Stir occasionally to keep the grains separate. Remove from the heat. Stir in the butter and leave to cool. Preheat the oven to gas mark 7, 425°F (220°C). Meanwhile roll out the pastry. Grease a 2 pt (1·1 litres) pie dish and line with the pastry. When the rice is cold, beat in the eggs, sugar, cinnamon and cream. Pour into the lined pie dish. Sprinkle with nutmeg and bake in the oven for 15 minutes, then reduce the heat to gas mark 5, 375°F (190°C). Bake for a further 30 minutes until the pastry is well risen and golden brown. Serve with cream or fruit.

# BAKED APPLES

The medieval fear and suspicion of uncooked fruit died hard since it was an obvious source of disease. During the sixteenth century, years of plague and pestilence were blamed on fruits. Not until the eighteenth century was washed fruit regarded as either a safe or a healthy food. Earlier, fruit was therefore cooked and enjoyed in tarts and pies.

You can invent your own stuffings for baked apples, including mixtures of fruit and nuts.

| | |
|---|---|
| 4–6 cooking apples (not too sour) | 2 tablespoons sultanas |
| 4 cloves for each apple | 4 oz (110 g) butter |
| 1 tablespoon dried dates *or* apricots *or* figs | 2 tablespoons sugar |

Preheat the oven to gas mark 4, 350°F (180°C). Wash and core the apples. Peel the top of each apple and stud each with 4 cloves. Chop the dried fruit and mix with the sultanas, half the butter and all the sugar. Fill the centre of each apple with this mixture. Put a small knob of butter on top of each apple and place on a baking tray. Cover the bottom of the tray with water and bake in the oven until the apples are soft (45 minutes–1 hour).

# APPLE FRITTERS

Here are two eighteenth-century batter recipes for coating thin rounds of peeled apples. Dip them in the batter and deep fry in oil until golden. Serve with sugar and a sweet sauce.

### RECIPE 1

| | |
|---|---|
| ½ pt (285 ml) ale *or* cider | 1–2 teaspoons sugar |
| 2 eggs, beaten | flour |
| grated nutmeg | |

Mix together the ale, eggs, nutmeg and sugar in a bowl. Beat in enough flour to make a thick, creamy batter. Allow to stand for 30 minutes before using.

### RECIPE 2

| | |
|---|---|
| ½ pt (285 ml) cream *or* milk | pinch of salt |
| small glass brandy *or* sherry | ½ teaspoon powdered ginger |
| 2 eggs, beaten | flour |

Mix together the cream, brandy, eggs, salt and ginger in a bowl. Beat in enough flour to make a thick, creamy batter. Allow to stand for 30 minutes before using.

# · ELDERFLOWER FRITTERS

The creamy white flowers of the elder appear in the hedgerows during May and June. If you are not using all your gathered blossom for winemaking, try these simple fritters for a taste of summer. Such fritters were very popular in the sixteenth and seventeenth centuries. Try the same batter with leaves of spinach, lettuce, bugloss or comfrey. Powdered spices or finely chopped herbs can be used to flavour the batter.

| | |
|---|---|
| 4 oz (110 g) flour | ½ pt (285 ml) batter liquid |
| pinch of salt | made from 7 fl oz (200 ml) |
| 1 egg | milk and 3 fl oz (85 ml) |
| elderflower sprigs | water |

Sift the flour with the salt in a bowl. Make a well in the centre and break in the egg. Add half of the liquid. Beat the flour into the centre gradually until it is well mixed with the egg and batter liquid. Add the rest of the liquid. Just before using, stir in an extra tablespoon of warm water. Dip the elderflower sprigs in the batter and deep fry in hot oil until golden. Serve with cream.

# FRUMENTY

Buttered cereals became popular in Tudor times. Oats, wheat, barley and rice were boiled in water, then mixed with butter. In London, this mixture could be bought by the dishful. Customers would take it home and reheat it with some sugar and spices.

In former times, frumenty was offered to strangers calling on Christmas Eve. In some parts of the country it is a dish for mid-Lent. Christmas frumenty is still eaten in many Yorkshire rural communities. Once finished, on New Year's Eve, no more would be made until the following year. In Suffolk, frumenty was put outside the door for the 'farisees' or fairies. In Cumberland and Northumberland, a generous knob of butter is stirred into the cooked wheat along with mixed spice, currants, sugar, cream and rum.

| | |
|---|---|
| kibbled (hulled and coarsely ground wheat) | dried fruit |
| | sugar |
| milk | spices |

Simmer the kibbled wheat in water until it begins to soften. Strain and cook for another 30 minutes with the rest of the ingredients.

# APPLE PIE

Apple pie without a cheese
Is like a kiss without a squeeze.

North Country saying

This recipe has continued to be used, almost without change, since medieval times.

| | |
|---|---|
| 1 lb (450 g) apples, peeled, cored and sliced | ½ teaspoon powdered cinnamon |
| 2 tablespoons currants | 2 tablespoons rosewater |
| 1 tablespoon chopped candied peel | 2 tablespoons sugar |
| 2 oz (60 g) butter | 8 oz (225 g) shortcrust pastry |
| 2–4 cloves | milk |

In a bowl, mix the apples, currants, peel, butter and spices. Put this mixture in a greased pie dish and pour a little rosewater over it. Sprinkle with sugar. Preheat the oven to gas mark 4, 350°F (180°C). Roll out the pastry. Dampen the edges of the pie dish and cover with the piecrust. Press down the edges with a fork and trim with a knife. Pierce the centre to allow the steam to escape. Brush with milk to glaze. Bake in the oven until the pastry is golden (about 30 minutes).

# SPICED PEARS

This dish was 'cried' at Bedford on the feast of St Simon and St Jude, 28 October.

| | |
|---|---|
| **6 Conference pears** | **1 piece cinnamon** |
| **1 pt (570 ml) sweet red wine** | **4–6 cloves** |

Peel the pears, halve and remove the cores. Put in a pan with the wine and spices. Stew gently until the pears are tender. Serve with cream or custard.

# SYLLABUB

In the sixteenth century, syllabub was a spiced drink made of milk with rum, port, brandy or wine, often served hot as a restorative. This curd of warm milk (for best results the cow was milked straight into the wine) became a favourite at any farm celebration. It could also include sherry, cider or ale according to the county.

A Somerset recipe of 1835 gives the ingredients as 'a pint of port and a pint of sherry or other white wine with sugar to taste. Milk the bowl full. In 20 minutes cover with clotted cream. Grate over nutmeg, put on pounded cinnamon and "non pareil comfits".'

In modern times it has tended to become a pudding made with thick cream. As such, it also makes the perfect topping for a trifle.

| | |
|---|---|
| **5 fl oz (140 ml) white wine** *or* **sherry** | **½ pt (285 ml) double cream** *or* **fresh curd cheese** |
| **1 tablespoon brandy** | **grated nutmeg** |
| **2 tablespoons sugar** | **grated lemon peel** |

Stir the wine, brandy and sugar together in a mixing bowl until the sugar has dissolved. Gradually beat in the cream and continue beating until the mixture thickens. Serve in glasses and sprinkle with nutmeg and a little finely grated lemon peel.

# Breads, Cakes & Dumplings

Pat-a-cake, pat-a-cake, baker's man,
Bake me a cake as fast as you can;
Pat it and prick it, and mark it with 'B',
Put it in the oven for Baby and me.

As the nursery rhyme suggests, the bakery was the centre of village cookery and for a small sum the baker would bake your bread, cake or even cook your pot roast.

Hundreds of 'feasten' and everyday cakes featured in the calendar of a century ago – Yorkshire parkin, Shrewsbury cakes, cowslip cake, gingerbread shapes, Cumberland currant pastry, Devon revel buns; each part of the country was noted for some speciality. It was said that enough cheesecakes were eaten at the Whitsun feast at Melton Mowbray to pave the whole town.

*See also the recipe for:*
Beef Stew with Dumplings

# SPICEBREAD

| | |
|---|---|
| 3½ lb (1·6 kg) flour | 8 oz (225 g) currants |
| pinch of salt | 8 oz (225 g) raisins |
| 1 teaspoon mixed spice powder | 4 oz (110 g) chopped peel |
| 8 oz (225 g) butter | 2 oz (60 g) fresh yeast |
| 4 oz (110 g) lard | 1 egg |
| 6 oz (170 g) sugar | warm milk |

Sift the flour into a mixing bowl with the salt and spice. Cut the butter and lard into pieces and rub into the flour. Add 5 oz (140 g) of the sugar and the dried fruit. Mix well. In a jug, cream together the yeast and the rest of the sugar. Add a cup of warm water and leave for 10 minutes for the yeast to ferment. Make a well in the centre of the flour and break in the egg. Pour in the yeast mixture and stir in the flour. Gradually add enough milk to make a smooth, pliable dough. Knead well for 10 minutes. Cover with a cloth and leave to rise in a warm place for 30 minutes.

While the bread is rising, preheat the oven to gas mark 7, 425°F (220°C). Grease two bread tins and divide up the dough. Bake in the oven until the bread is well done (40 minutes–1 hour). It should sound hollow when the underside is tapped. Leave to cool on wire racks.

# BEGGAR'S PUDDING

This spicy bread pudding comes from the former county of Huntingdonshire, now part of Cambridgeshire. You can vary the ingredients to suit what you have available in the way of fruit and spices.

| | |
|---|---|
| 8 oz (225 g) stale bread | 1 teaspoon grated nutmeg |
| ½ pt (285 ml) milk | 1 teaspoon powdered mace |
| 1 tablespoon currants | 1 teaspoon powdered cinnamon |
| 1 tablespoon raisins *or* sultanas | 1 teaspoon powdered ginger |
| 1 tablespoon chopped mixed peel | 1 egg |
| 2 oz (60 g) butter, cut in pieces | 4 tablespoons milk |
| 4 oz (110 g) sugar | |

Break up the bread and put it in a bowl. Pour over it the milk and leave to soak. Preheat the oven to gas mark 4, 350°F (180°C). Squeeze the bread and beat with a fork. Add the dried fruit, butter, sugar and spices. In a separate bowl, beat together the egg and the 4 tablespoons of milk. Beat into the bread mixture. Put in a greased bread or cake tin and bake in the oven until the pudding is set (about 45 minutes), when a fork should come out cleanly. Leave to cool on a wire rack.

# ELIZABETHAN TOAST

Enriched toasts were a favourite medieval snack and they offer scope for
your own experimentation with ingredients, including herbs and spices.

| | |
|---|---|
| 8 oz (225 g) lamb's kidneys | pinch of powdered ginger |
| 2 tablespoons dripping *or* butter | ½ teaspoon sugar |
| 2 egg yolks | 1 tablespoon rosewater |
| pinch of powdered cinnamon | 2–4 slices of toast |

Clean the kidneys and chop them. Heat the fat in a pan and gently fry the
kidneys, beating in the egg during this process. Before the eggs are set, mix
in the spices, sugar and rosewater. Spread on toast while still hot. Serve
immediately.

# HOT CROSS BUNS

Hot cross buns! Hot cross buns!
One a penny, two a penny,
Hot cross buns!

Hot cross buns are both marked and filled with the symbolism of Easter, for
the spices in them represent the spiced vinegar that was offered to the
crucified Jesus. These spiced buns well repay the effort of home baking.

| | |
|---|---|
| 2 tablespoons sugar | 3 oz (85 g) currants |
| 1 tablespoon dried yeast | 2 oz (60 g) chopped mixed peel |
| 1 lb (450 g) flour | 2 tablespoons warm milk |
| 1 teaspoon salt | 1 egg, beaten |
| ½ teaspoon powdered cinnamon | 2 oz (60 g) butter, melted |
| ½ teaspoon powdered ginger | 4 oz (110 g) shortcrust pastry |
| ½ teaspoon grated nutmeg | |

*for the glaze*
2 tablespoons sugar
2 tablespoons water

Preheat the oven to a low heat for warming the dough. Stir 1 teaspoon of
the sugar into ¼ pt (140 ml) of warm water. Sprinkle on top the dried
yeast, stir and leave to form a froth for 10 minutes. Meanwhile sift the flour
with the salt and spices into a mixing bowl. Add the rest of the sugar,
currants and peel. Stir together and make a well in the middle. Pour into
this the yeast mixture, milk, egg and melted butter. Mix together with a
wooden spoon to make a stiff dough, adding a little more milk if necessary.

Knead the dough for 5 minutes until it is smooth and springy. Cover with a cloth and leave in a warm place for the dough to rise and double its size (about 1 hour).

Turn out the dough and knead again for 2–3 minutes. Divide the mixture into 12 equal portions. Roll each portion into a ball and press slightly to make a flat bun. Put the buns on greased baking sheets. Cover and leave to rise again in a warm place for 30 minutes.

Heat the oven to gas mark 7, 425°F (220°C). Roll out the pastry and make into thin strips. Moisten the strips with water and press onto the uncooked buns to make the shape of a cross. If no pastry is available, simply make a deep cross with a knife on each bun. Bake in the oven until the buns are golden (about 15 minutes).

Meanwhile heat the sugar and water until the sugar is dissolved. Brush each bun with this glazing liquid as soon as they come out of the oven (honey is also suitable for this purpose). Leave to cool on a wire rack.

# GINGER CAKE

There must be a different gingerbread or ginger cake recipe for every town in the country. Here is a recipe from Yorkshire that is sufficient for two cakes. To give extra spice, some cooks add a pinch of chilli powder or even Worcestershire sauce along with the spices. Substitute some currants and lemon peel for the crystallized ginger and walnuts, and you have what is known as Cumberland cake.

| | |
|---|---|
| 8 oz (225 g) flour | 4 tablespoons black treacle *or* |
| pinch of salt | golden syrup |
| 1 teaspoon bicarbonate of soda | 1 egg |
| 1 teaspoon powdered cinnamon | 2 tablespoons milk |
| 2 teaspoons powdered ginger | 1 tablespoon finely chopped |
| 4 oz (110 g) butter | crystallized ginger |
| 4 oz (110 g) sugar | 1 tablespoon chopped walnuts |

Preheat the oven to gas mark 4, 350°F (180°C). Sift the flour with the salt, bicarbonate of soda and spices. Put the butter in a pan with the sugar and treacle. Melt together over a low heat, stirring well. Allow to cool a little, then beat in the egg and milk. Pour the mixture into the spiced flour and beat together until smooth. Stir in the ginger and nuts. Line the base and sides of a bread tin or tins with greaseproof paper smeared with butter. Put the mixture in, and bake in the oven until the cake has risen and is firm to the touch (about 45 minutes), when a fork should come out cleanly. Leave to cool on a wire rack.

## GINGER PARKIN

| | |
|---|---|
| 1 lb (450 g) oats | 4 oz (110 g) chopped mixed peel |
| pinch of salt | 8 oz (225 g) butter |
| ½ oz (15 g) powdered ginger | 8 oz (225 g) sugar |
| pinch of powdered mace | 4 oz (110 g) black treacle |
| pinch of grated nutmeg | 1 egg, beaten |

Preheat the oven to gas mark 4, 350°F (180°C). Combine the oats, salt, spices and peel in a bowl. Melt the butter in a pan with the sugar and treacle. Mix well and pour onto the oat mixture. Add the beaten egg and mix well. Pour into a greased tin. Bake in the oven until the parkin is firm to the touch (45 minutes–1 hour). Leave to cool on a wire rack and keep in an airtight tin. Parkin is best eaten a few days after cooking.

## TWELFTH NIGHT CAKE

In Worcestershire, Herefordshire and Gloucestershire, Twelfth Night fires were lit in the wheatfields. Around these fires farmers, servants and friends drank a toast to the next harvest in mulled cider. Other refreshment on these occasions was the rich Twelfth Night cake, a piece of which was put on the head of a bull for him to toss in the air.

> Fill your cups, my merry men all!
> For here is the best ox in the stall,
> Oh! He is the best ox, don't make no mistake,
> So let us crown him with Twelfth Night cake!

| | |
|---|---|
| 8 oz (225 g) butter | ½ teaspoon baking powder |
| 8 oz (225 g) sugar | 8 oz (225 g) currants |
| 1 teaspoon powdered ginger | 8 oz (225 g) sultanas |
| 1 teaspoon powdered cinnamon | 2 oz (60 g) almonds, blanched and |
| 1 teaspoon powdered coriander seed |    sliced |
| 2–4 allspice berries, pounded | 2 oz (60 g) candied peel |
| 5 eggs, beaten | 2 teaspoons grated lemon peel |
| 8 oz (225 g) flour | |

Preheat the oven to gas mark ½, 250°F (120°C). Cream together the butter and sugar. Beat in the spices, and then the eggs. Sift together the flour and baking powder. Gradually add the flour mixture to the fat and egg mixture, and stir well. Add the currants, sultanas, almonds, candied peel and lemon peel. Beat the mixture well. Line the bottom and sides of an 8 in (20 cm) cake tin with greaseproof paper which has been smeared with butter. Turn the cake mixture into the tin and smooth the top. Bake in the middle of the oven until the cake is golden and well cooked (4 hours), when a fork should come out cleanly. Leave to cool on a wire rack.

Before the cake is used on Twelfth Night, coat the top with marzipan and icing. The cake may be made a month before it is needed.

## SIMNEL CAKE

Known as Mothering Sunday, the fourth Sunday in Lent was a holiday for apprentices and girls in service, who were allowed to go home to visit their mothers with a bunch of violets and a Simnel cake or small gift. Shrewsbury, Devizes and Bury are still famous for their Simnel cakes. Spiced ale or bragot was also drunk in Lancashire on Simnel Sunday.

| | |
|---|---|
| 4 oz (110 g) lard | 12 almonds, blanched and sliced |
| 4 oz (110 g) sugar | 1 tablespoon brandy *or* sherry |
| 2 eggs, beaten | 1 tablespoon cider vinegar *or* malt |
| 6 oz (170 g) flour | vinegar |
| ¼ teaspoon bicarbonate of soda | ¼ teaspoon grated nutmeg |
| 1 tablespoon milk | ¼ teaspoon salt |
| 4 oz (110 g) currants | 3 allspice berries, pounded |
| 4 oz (110 g) sultanas | 4 oz (110 g) marzipan |
| 4 oz (110 g) chopped mixed peel | |

Preheat the oven to gas mark ½, 250°F (120°C). Cut the lard into pieces in a mixing bowl and cream together with the sugar. Beat in the eggs. Gradually stir in the flour. Dissolve the bicarbonate of soda in the milk and stir in. Add the fruit, peel and almonds. Stir in the brandy, vinegar, nutmeg, salt and allspice. Mix together well. Line the base and sides of a 6 in (15 cm) cake tin with greaseproof paper which has been smeared with butter. Spoon in the cake mixture. Smooth the top and bake in the oven until the cake is set and golden on top (about 3½ hours). Test in the centre with a fork, which should come out cleanly. Leave the cake to cool on a wire rack.

Next day, cover with marzipan. The cake may then be iced and decorated like any other festive cake.

# SEED CAKE

One to rot and one to grow, one for the pigeon and one for the crow.

Farmers in Yorkshire and East Anglia never began ploughing on a Friday, a day when soil should not be disturbed with iron tools. This memory of Friday as a holy day in the old Christian calendar is blended with early man's reverence for iron. In the South a piece of cake from the ploughman's elevenses might be dropped in the furrows for good luck and a good harvest. In Elizabethan times, the sower traditionally received the rewards of 'seedcake, pasties and frumentie pot'. The cake was often called a siblett cake.

| | |
|---|---|
| 4 oz (110 g) butter | ½ teaspoon baking powder |
| 4 oz (110 g) sugar | 1 tablespoon chopped mixed peel |
| 2 eggs, well beaten | 2 teaspoons caraway seed |
| 6 oz (170 g) flour | 1 tablespoon milk |

Preheat the oven to gas mark 4, 350°F (180°C). Warm the butter a little. Cream the butter and sugar together with a fork. Beat in the eggs until they are well mixed. Sift the flour with the baking powder and gradually stir into the mixture. Add the mixed peel, seeds and milk and mix together well. Line a 6 in (15 cm) diameter cake tin with greaseproof paper which has been lightly smeared with butter. Spoon the mixture into the cake tin, smooth the top and bake in the oven until the cake is set (about 1 hour). Test with a fork, which should come out cleanly from the centre. Take care not to open the oven in the early stages of baking, or the cake will sink. Leave to cool on a wire rack.

# BANBURY CAKES

Ride a cock-horse to Banbury Cross
To see a fine lady upon a white horse;
With rings on her fingers and bells on her toes,
She shall have music wherever she goes.

| | |
|---|---|
| 3 oz (85 g) butter | grated nutmeg |
| 3 oz (85 g) chopped mixed peel | ¾ tablespoon clear honey |
| 3 oz (85 g) sultanas | 12 oz (340 g) puff pastry |
| ½ teaspoon powdered cinnamon | milk |
| ½ teaspoon powdered ginger | |

Preheat the oven to gas mark 7, 425°F (220°C). Soften the butter and beat with a fork. Stir in the peel, sultanas, spices and honey. Roll out the pastry on a floured surface. Cut 8 rounds to fit the depressions in a greased tart tray and 8 rounds to cover. Put a spoonful of the spice mixture into each of the pastry rounds. Moisten the edges and cover with the pastry tops. Seal the edges carefully. Flatten each cake slightly and make a small slit in the top to allow any steam to escape. Brush the tops with milk to glaze. Bake in the oven for 15 minutes. Leave to cool on a wire rack before removing from the tart tray.

# YORKSHIRE CURD TART

On the farm, the curd cheese for this recipe used to be made from beastings – the first milk (colostrum) from a newly calved cow. These tarts are excellent with apple sauce or a small piece of apple pie.

| | |
|---|---|
| 8 oz (225 g) curd cheese | 3 eggs, beaten |
| 2 tablespoons sugar | 2 oz (60 g) butter |
| 2 tablespoons currants *or* sultanas | 1 tablespoon rum *or* brandy |
| 1 teaspoon finely grated lemon | 12 oz (340 g) shortcrust pastry |
|   peel | grated nutmeg |

Preheat the oven to gas mark 4, 350°F (180°C). Break up the cheese with a fork in a bowl. Add the sugar, currants, lemon peel and eggs. Melt the butter in a pan and stir in the rum. Add to the cheese mixture. Roll out the pastry and line a greased 8 in (20 cm) flan tin with it, or cut up to make rounds for 24 small tarts. Fill with the cheese mixture and sprinkle with nutmeg. Bake in the oven until the filling is firm (about 25–30 minutes).

# SPICED MACAROONS

4 oz (110 g) finely ground almonds | 1 clove, pounded finely
8 oz (225 g) sugar | 2 egg whites
1 oz (30 g) rice flour | 9 almonds, blanched, skinned and
¼ teaspoon powdered cinnamon | cut in half lengthways to make 2
¼ teaspoon grated lemon peel | flat halves

Preheat the oven to gas mark 4, 350°F (180°C). Mix the ground almonds, sugar and rice flour with the spices. In a separate bowl, beat the egg whites until stiff. Use a metal spoon to fold the almond mixture into the egg whites. Line two baking trays with greased baking paper or rice paper. Put 16–18 spoonsful of the mixture onto the paper, allowing enough space for the macaroons to spread. Put a split almond in the middle of each. Bake in the oven until the macaroons are golden (25–30 minutes). Allow to cool on a wire rack. If the macaroons are on rice paper simply cut round and leave a rice paper base for each one.

# HERB DUMPLINGS

Davy Davy Dumpling,
Boil him in the pot;
Sugar him and butter him,
And eat him while he's hot.

3 oz (85 g) flour | ½ teaspoon sage
¼ teaspoon baking powder | ½ teaspoon thyme
1 teaspoon salt | ½ teaspoon marjoram
½ teaspoon freshly ground | 1 oz (30 g) shredded suet
pepper | milk
½ teaspoon rosemary

Sift the flour with the baking powder, salt and pepper into a bowl. Stir in the herbs and suet. Add enough milk to make a stiff dough. Divide into 8 portions and shape each portion into a ball. Allow to boil in a stew or a pan of water for 30 minutes.

The herbs may be varied to suit what is available or to blend with certain dishes. Serve with a stew or savoury dish or 'Sugar him and butter him, and eat him while he's hot'!

# Drinks

On New Year's Eve, the annual supper for bellringers in Cambridgeshire included a hot drink of beer, spirits, eggs, sugar, nutmeg and milk drunk from a cow's horn. This was very similar to the Christmas wassail drink in other parts of the country. Spiced elderberry wine was the custom in Suffolk, accompanied by special cakes.

## SACK POSSET

Sack is the sixteenth-century word for any dry white wine from south-west Europe, especially sherry. The possets of the preceding century were originally intended for medicinal purposes, but they came to be used as restorative drinks for cold nights and wintry days. Until the turn of the century, sack posset was a common wedding drink in country regions.

| 1 pt (570 ml) milk | grated nutmeg |
| 2 wholemeal biscuits | ½ pt (285 ml) sherry *or* |
| 1–2 teaspoons sugar | dry white wine |

Put the milk into a large pan and crumble the biscuits into it. Add the sugar and nutmeg and allow to simmer for 5 minutes. Cool, and pour the sherry into the mixture. Serve hot or cold.

# ORANGE POSSET

| | |
|---|---|
| 1 pt (570 ml) milk | 2 tablespoons ground almonds |
| 1 cup breadcrumbs | a few juniper berries |
| grated peel of ½ orange | 2 tablespoons brandy |
| ½ pt (285 ml) sweet red wine | 2 teaspoons sugar |
| juice of ½ orange | |

Put the milk in a pan and add the breadcrumbs and orange peel. Heat together gently for 5 minutes. Add the rest of the ingredients and mix well. Strain before using. Serve hot or cold.

# WHITE CAUDLE

Hot spiced gruels were used medicinally in the Middle Ages. This eighteenth-century recipe fortifies the caudle with wine to make a nourishing posset.

| | |
|---|---|
| 1½ pt (850 ml) water | sugar |
| 4 tablespoons oats | grated nutmeg |
| 2 blades mace | dry white wine |
| 1 strip lemon peel | |

Put the water in a large pan with the oats, mace and lemon peel. Boil together for 15 minutes, stirring occasionally. Strain through a coarse sieve. Add sugar, nutmeg and wine to taste.

# EGG CAUDLE

The medieval egg-thickened caudles of wine or ale continued to be enjoyed as substantial breakfast or supper drinks until well into the eighteenth century. An innovation was the tea caudle, which developed with the new habit of tea-drinking.

| | |
|---|---|
| 1 pt (570 ml) strong green tea | 2 egg yolks |
| ½ pt (285 ml) dry white wine *or* sherry | sugar |
| | grated nutmeg |

Put the tea in a pan with the wine, egg yolks, sugar and grated nutmeg to taste. Heat together gently.

# WHEY WIG

**chopped fresh herbs**
**buttermilk** *or* **yogurt**

Mixed chopped fresh herbs, such as sage or mint, with a glass of buttermilk or thinned yogurt. Allow to stand for 15 minutes before serving.

# LOVING CUP

Here is an ideal eighteenth-century punch for an engagement or wedding party

| | |
|---|---|
| 1 pt (570 ml) sweet red dessert wine | 1 glass brandy |
| 1 pt (570 ml) Madeira | juice and sliced peel of 1 lemon |
| 1 pt (570 ml) port | 1 tablespoon sugar |
| 1 bottle champagne | a few cloves |
| | a few sticks cinnamon |

Mix the ingredients well. Strain and serve with ice.

# LAMB'S WOOL

Wassail! Wassail! All over the town,
Our toast it is white and our ale it is brown,
Our bowl it is made of the white maple tree;
With the wassailing bowl we'll drink to thee!

Wassail (from the Old English *was hel* – be of good health) describes a village custom which has almost died out. Originally a fertility ritual involving the villagers and their fruit trees, wassailers went about with large, iron-handled wooden bowls decorated with evergreen twigs and ribbons and filled with 'lamb's wool'. This steaming brew of hot ale, roasted crab apples, toast, nutmeg, sugar and eggs would be offered to anyone they met. Father Christmas was often pictured in old prints as a jolly figure bearing the wassail bowl.

Here is a hot punch of the same name from Oxford. This university ale cup is obviously based on the traditional wassail cup. The 'toast' in the song refers to the custom of floating a piece of spiced toast on the top of the punch.

| | |
|---|---|
| 2 pt (1·1 litres) ale | 2 apples, peeled, cored |
| 1 pt (570 ml) white wine | and sliced |
| grated nutmeg | butter |
| 1 stick cinnamon | pounded cloves |
| | sugar |

Heat the ale and wine together. On no account let the mixture boil. Add the nutmeg and cinnamon. Slice the apples thinly and fry them in butter until lightly golden. Roll the fried apple in the pounded cloves and sugar. Put the mixture in a large, deep bowl and float the apple slices on the top.

## CAMBRIDGE ALE CUP

| | |
|---|---|
| 2 pt (1·1 litres) water | juice and grated peel of |
| 6 cloves | 1 lemon |
| 2 sticks cinnamon | 3 pt (1·7 litres) ale |
| 2 blades mace | ½ pt (285 ml) sherry |
| 1 tablespoon sugar | thin toast |
| | grated nutmeg |

Simmer the water with the spices for 30 minutes. Strain into a large bowl and add the sugar, lemon, ale and sherry. Heat just before serving. This cup was traditionally garnished with small pieces of thin toast sprinkled with grated nutmeg.

## HEREFORD CIDER CUP

| | |
|---|---|
| 2 pt (1·1 litres) cider | 2 tablespoons sugar |
| juice and grated peel of | 2 glasses brandy |
| ½ lemon | sprigs of borage |

Mix the cider, lemon, sugar and brandy in a large bowl. Serve with ice and sprigs of borage.

# HERB TEAS

In her *Complete Cottage Cookery* (1859), Esther Copley has a section on 'frugality and cheap cookery'. Here she offers help to those finding the price of Indian and China tea, which was relatively much more expensive then than today, a little beyond their means. She simply uses common sense and good country lore and suggests that we might just as easily drink hot teas which are free.

Those who can ill afford to buy foreign tea may easily stock themselves from their own gardens thus – gather strawberry leaves while young and tender, pick off the stalks and dry them in an airy but shady place; when sufficient quantity is collected and the whole is perfectly dry, it may be kept in a canister or bottle, as other tea, and used in the same manner. [. . .] Another substitute is hawthorn leaves, picked and dried, and mixed with one tenth part each of balm and green sage. Other ingredients for making teas are agrimony, wild marjoram, red rose petals, cowslip flowers and blackcurrant leaves – all to be cut small and mixed as they are gathered. When all are dried, store and use as above.

A simple recipe for herb teas consists of 1–2 teaspoons of dried herbs per cup or 1 tablespoon of fresh herbs per cup. Put the herbs in a warm earthenware teapot and pour on boiling water. Stir, and let the tea infuse for 5 minutes. Strain and serve in tea cups or thick glasses.

# Pastes, Pâtés, Pickles & Preserves

The knowledge of pickling is very essential in a family. Stone jars are the
most proper for all sorts of pickles, for though they are expensive in the first
purchase, yet they will, in the end, be found much cheaper than earthen
vessels, through which, it has been found by experience, salt and vinegar
will penetrate, especially when put in hot. Be careful never to put your
fingers in to take the pickles out, as it will soon spoil them; but always make
use of a spoon upon those occasions.

General Observations on Pickling, *Mrs Cole's Cookery*, 1791

As a general rule, never heat a vinegar mixture in an aluminium pan.

## POTTED SHRIMPS

Since the eighteenth century, surplus shrimps have been potted and sold
at many coastal resorts.

1 lb 2oz (500 g) freshly boiled
   shrimps, shelled
½ teaspoon powdered mace
pinch of powdered ginger

pinch of chilli powder
freshly ground pepper
6 oz (170 g) clarified butter

Beat the shrimps with the spices and pepper to taste. Melt half the butter in a pan and stir the seasoned shrimps into it. Remove from the heat and press into small pots. Pour more melted butter over to cover them while they are still warm. Store in a cool place. Serve with toast and slices of lemon.

## POTTED SPRATS

| | |
|---|---|
| 1 lb (450 g) sprats | ¼ teaspoon powdered mace |
| 5 fl oz (140 ml) white vinegar | 2 bay leaves |
| ½ pt (285 ml) water | 5 peppercorns |
| ½ teaspoon salt | 2–4 oz (60–110 g) butter, |
| ¼ teaspoon freshly ground pepper | melted |

Remove the heads from the sprats and gut them. Wash, and pat dry. Place in a pan and pour over them the vinegar and water. Season with the salt and spices. Stew until the sprats are tender. Allow to cool, lift out the sprats and allow to drain. Pack tightly in small pots and pour melted butter over them to cover. Store in a cool, dry place.

## POTTED TROUT

Potted fish became a fashionable dish in the seventeenth century at the tables of the wealthy. This dish ousted the cold fish pies which only survived in a few regional versions. Here is a recipe from Cumberland. Carp and tench may also be potted in the same way.

| | |
|---|---|
| 2 trout | ¼ teaspoon mustard seeds |
| vinegar | 6 cloves |
| butter | grated nutmeg |
| juice of ½ lemon | ½ teaspoon powdered mace |
| 2 bay leaves | pinch of chilli powder |
| 6 peppercorns | clarified butter |

Preheat the oven to gas mark 1, 275°F (140°C). Clean and wash the trout well in cold water and vinegar. Dry with a cloth. Grease an ovenproof dish with butter and rub each trout with butter. Put the trout in the dish, with the backs uppermost. Sprinkle with lemon juice and bay leaf. Grind together the peppercorns, mustard seed and cloves. Add the nutmeg, mace and chilli. Sprinkle these spices over the fish. Cover with a piece of greaseproof paper or foil smeared with butter. Bake in the oven for 2 hours. Allow to cool. Remove the bay leaves and pound the fish well. Put in pots and cover with melted butter. Store in a cool, dry place.

## NEWCASTLE POTTED SALMON

Beer was the secret of the famous Newcastle potted salmon which came from the river Tweed. The fish were carried 60 miles by packhorse to Shields, and simmered in strong beer and pickled and salted before being sent to London and other ports.

| | |
|---|---|
| 2 lb (900 g) salmon | 1 teaspoon powdered mace |
| 2 pt (1·1 litres) water | 6 cloves, pounded |
| 3 pt (1·7 litres) strong beer | freshly ground pepper |
| 2 teaspoons salt | clarified butter |
| 4 bay leaves | |

Simmer the salmon in water, beer, salt and bay leaves for 1 hour. Next day remove the fish and drain. Pound in a bowl and add the spices. Mix well together and put in pots. Cover with melted butter. Store in a cool, dry place.

## POTTED BEEF

Like potted fish, potted meats in jelly became very popular in Elizabethan times. They can of course be potted in butter instead.

| | |
|---|---|
| 1 lb (450 g) shin of beef | small bunch of herbs |
| 1 pig's trotter | ¾ pt (425 ml) stock *or* water |
| 1 small onion, stuck with 4 cloves | 1 teaspoon salt |
| 1 blade mace | freshly ground pepper |

Preheat the oven to gas mark 2, 300°F (150°C). Cut the beef into small pieces. Make cuts in the trotter with a sharp knife. Put all the meat in an ovenproof dish with the onion, mace and herbs. Cover with the stock and bring to the boil. Turn down the heat and simmer gently. Remove any scum and season with salt and pepper to taste. Cover and cook in the oven for 3 hours.

Remove the onion, mace and herbs and discard. Skin the trotter and separate the pork meat from the bone. Discard the bones. Shred the beef and pork finely. Put the shredded meat in a bowl and strain over it enough stock to just cover. Allow to cool. The stock should set to a nice jelly. Store in a cool, dry place.

## MARBLE VEAL

It was discovered in the eighteenth century that meat could be made to keep better if it was finely minced and beaten with butter. Many meats were potted in this way – usually two different meats combined. They were beaten to a paste and put in the pot in layers to create a marbled effect when cut. Potted veal and tongue was known as marble veal.

Mince together equal quantities of cooked veal and tongue. Beat with a little fresh butter and spices such as mace, nutmeg and pepper. Press firmly into pots to exclude any air. Keep in a cool, dry place.

## PORK AND HERB PASTE

From the time of the Industrial Revolution, coarse pastes and potted meats were put in small pots and sold commercially. Today, most people have only experienced the minute little pots which are now sold under the title of 'paste'. On the continent, the tradition of home-made potted meats has continued, of which the various pâtés are probably the most familiar.

Pastes or pâtés will keep for a week or two in a cool place. If you wish to preserve them longer, cover with a layer of clarified butter while they are still hot and store in the refrigerator.

This traditional English recipe uses baking as part of the preservation process and the end result is not unlike a continental pâté.

| | |
|---|---|
| 1 lb (450 g) belly pork | 8 oz (225 g) spinach |
| 8 oz (225 g) rabbit meat | 4 oz (110 g) dandelion leaves *or* |
| 4 oz (110 g) chicken livers | chervil |
| 1 medium onion, finely chopped | 2 oz (60 g) chopped parsley |
| 2 cloves garlic, finely chopped | 2 oz (60 g) chopped mixed herbs |
| 1 teaspoon salt | 1 egg, beaten |
| 2 peppercorns | juice of ½ lemon |
| 6 juniper berries | |

Mince the pork and rabbit meat and chop the liver finely. Put in a bowl and beat together with a fork. Beat in the onion and garlic. Add the salt. Grind the peppercorns and juniper berries and beat in. Blanch the spinach and dandelion in boiling water for 2 minutes. Drain well and chop. Beat into the meat with the rest of the herbs. Stir in the egg and lemon juice and mix well together. Turn on the oven to gas mark 4, 350°F (180°C). Put the mixture into a greased ovenproof dish and cover with foil. Put in a roasting pan half filled with water and bake in the oven for 1¼ hours. Allow to cool before storing in a cool, dry place.

## CHICKEN PASTE

| | |
|---|---|
| 1 lb (450 g) uncooked chicken meat | 4 peppercorns |
| 8 oz (225 g) bacon, with rind removed | ¼ teaspoon grated nutmeg |
| 4 oz (110 g) chicken livers | ½ cup dry white wine |
| 1 onion, finely chopped | 2 tablespoons chopped parsley |
| 2 cloves of garlic, finely chopped | 2 tablespoons chopped tarragon *or* other fresh herb |
| 1 teaspoon salt | 1 egg, beaten |

Preheat the oven to gas mark 4, 350°F (180°C). Mince the chicken and bacon and chop the liver finely. Put in a bowl and beat together. Beat in the onion, garlic and salt. Grind the peppercorns and add to the mixture with the nutmeg. Stir in the rest of the ingredients and mix well. Put the mixture in a greased ovenproof dish and cover with foil. Put in a roasting pan which is half filled with water. Bake in the oven for 1¼ hours. Allow to cool before storing.

## RABBIT PASTE

| | |
|---|---|
| 1 lb (450 g) uncooked rabbit meat | ½ teaspoon powdered mace |
| 8 oz (225 g) fatty belly pork | 1 tablespoon chopped parsley |
| rabbit liver and heart | 2 teaspoons chopped sage |
| 1–2 cloves of garlic, finely chopped | 2 teaspoons chopped thyme |
| 1 teaspoon salt | 1 egg, beaten |
| 4 peppercorns | ½ cup dry red wine |
| 6 juniper berries | 4–6 rashers unsmoked bacon |

Preheat the oven to gas mark 4, 350°F (180°C). Mince the rabbit and the belly pork. Chop the liver and heart. Put in a bowl and beat together with a fork. Beat in the garlic and salt. Grind the peppercorns and juniper berries together and beat them in. Stir in the rest of the ingredients except the bacon and mix well. Put the mixture in a greased ovenproof dish and cover with the bacon rashers. Cover the top with foil. Put the dish in a roasting pan which is half filled with water and bake in the oven for 1¼–1½ hours. Allow to cool before storing in a cool, dry place.

## POTTED RABBIT

| | |
|---|---|
| 1 rabbit, including liver and heart | 1 small onion, finely chopped |
| 6 allspice berries | 1 teaspoon salt |
| 6 peppercorns | 8 oz (225 g) butter |
| 2 blades of mace | ½ teaspoon chilli powder |
| 6 cloves | clarified butter |

Cut the rabbit into small pieces and put in a pan with the spices, onion and salt. Add ½ pt (285 ml) of water and cook together slowly until the rabbit is tender, adding more water if necessary. Allow the meat to cool and strain off the liquid, which can be used for stock or gravy. Take the meat from the bones and mince finely, together with the spices. Beat together with the butter and chilli powder and press firmly into pots. Cover with a little melted clarified butter. Store in a cool, dry place.

## PICKLED RED CABBAGE

A recipe which has hardly changed over the centuries, pickled red cabbage is excellent with hot and cold dishes.

| | |
|---|---|
| red cabbage | mace |
| salt | allspice berries |
| white wine vinegar | peppercorns |
| cloves | |

Wash, trim and slice the cabbage. Put in a dish and sprinkle salt over it. Cover with another dish and allow to stand for 24 hours. Put in a colander and drain, then put into clean, dry pickle jars. Pour in enough white wine vinegar to cover the cabbage. Now carefully pour off all the vinegar into a pan. Add a few cloves, mace, allspice berries and peppercorns. Bring the mixture to the boil. Allow to cool a little, then pour back over the cabbage in the jars while still hot. Seal the jars immediately. When cool, store in a cool, dry place. Allow to mature for 2 months before using.

## PICKLED CUCUMBER

| | |
|---|---|
| 2½ lb (1·1 kg) cucumbers | 2 teaspoons mustard seeds *or* |
| 1 large onion, sliced | peppercorns |
| 1 tablespoon salt | 2 cloves |
| white wine vinegar | 1 blade mace |
| 4 oz (110 g) sugar | small piece of horseradish root |

Do not peel the cucumbers but wash them and wipe them dry. Cut into slices. Put on a dish and sprinkle with the onion and salt. Cover with another dish and leave to stand for 4–6 hours. Drain, and put the cucumber and onion in clean, dry pickle jars. Pour in enough vinegar to cover. Carefully pour off the vinegar into a pan. Add the sugar and spices. Heat gently until the sugar has dissolved. Bring to the boil and turn off the heat. Allow to cool a little, then pour the liquid over the cucumber in the jars while still hot. Seal the jars immediately. When cool, store in a cool, dry place. Allow to mature for 2 months before using.

## PICKLED NASTURTIUM SEEDS

Many people prefer these to capers. The seeds of nasturtium (*Tropaeolum majus*) are more pungent than the buds after pickling.

| | |
|---|---|
| nasturtium seeds | 2 cloves |
| ½ pt (285 ml) pale | 1 bay leaf |
| vinegar | 1 teaspoon salt |
| 2 peppercorns | |

Put the vinegar in a pan and add the peppercorns, cloves, bay leaf and salt. Bring to the boil. Remove from the heat and leave to infuse for 2 hours. Strain, and put the spiced vinegar in small jars or bottles. Put in the nasturtium fruits as you gather them, while they are still young and green. Fill the jar almost to the top and seal. Keep for a month before use.

A variation of this recipe uses a slice of onion or shallot with a blade of mace and salt.

# GOOSEBERRY CHUTNEY

| | |
|---|---|
| 3 lb (1·3 kg) gooseberries | 4 allspice berries, pounded |
| 1 large onion, finely chopped | grated nutmeg |
| ½ pt (285 ml) water | 2 teaspoons salt |
| 12 oz (340 g) sultanas *or* | 8 oz (225 g) sugar |
| chopped dates | 1 pt (570 ml) vinegar |
| 2 teaspoons powdered ginger | |

Preheat the oven to a low heat and heat the chutney jars and lids. Wash the gooseberries and top and tail them. Drain and put in a preserving pan with the onions and water. Simmer for 20 minutes, adding more water if necessary to prevent burning. Stir in the dried fruit, spices, salt, sugar and vinegar. Simmer together gently until the chutney is thick, which may take some time. Spoon the hot chutney into hot jars and seal immediately. Store in a cool, dry place for at least a month before using.

# PICCALILLI

This traditional mixed-vegetable mustard pickle first appeared in the eighteenth century under the name 'piccalillo' or 'Indian pickle'.

| | |
|---|---|
| 1 lb (450 g) pickling onions | 2 tablespoons flour |
| 1 cucumber | 4 oz (110 g) sugar |
| 1 small cauliflower | 2 tablespoons mustard powder |
| 8 oz (225 g) green tomatoes | 1 tablespoon turmeric powder |
| 8 oz (225 g) marrow | 2 pt (1·1 litres) malt vinegar *or* |
| 2 tablespoons salt | red wine vinegar |

Cut the vegetables in small pieces, leaving very small onions whole. Put in a bowl and sprinkle with salt. Cover with a dish and leave for 24 hours. Drain off any liquid. Next day put some pickling jars – enough to hold about 6 lb (2·7 kg) – and their lids in the oven to warm on a low heat. Mix the flour, sugar, mustard and turmeric and put in a saucepan. Add a little vinegar to make a paste. Gradually add the rest of the vinegar. Bring to the boil over a gentle heat and stir until the liquid thickens. Add the vegetables and simmer for 5 minutes. Put into the hot jars and seal immediately. Allow to cool before storing in a cool, dry place. Allow the pickle to mature for 2 months before using.

# HERB VINEGAR

Herb vinegars are useful for making salad dressings, marinades, basting and other sauces, and for mixing with mustard powder. Use either white wine vinegar or cider vinegar. The strong flavour of malt vinegar can only be matched by garlic or mint.

> **6 oz (170 g) fresh herbs (sage,**
> **rosemary, mint, basil, chervil,**
> **borage, rue, etc.)**
> **1 pt (570 ml) vinegar**

The herbs should be picked before flowering. Wash the leaves and beat gently with a wooden spoon to bruise so that they will aromatize the vinegar. Put in a preserving jar and cover with the vinegar. Cover with a cloth and allow to steep for 2 weeks in a cool, dark place. Strain into bottles. Before sealing, drop a fresh sprig of one of the herbs in each bottle. Allow to mature in a cool, dark place for a month before using.

Herb vinegars are ideal for your own experiments. Spices such as clove and mace will change the flavour. Pieces of lemon peel and a small amount of chopped chives are very good with basil, marjoram, thyme or savory vinegars.

# HOME-MADE MUSTARD

| | |
|---|---|
| 1 tablespoon black mustard seeds | 1 teaspoon finely chopped thyme |
| 1 tablespoon white mustard seeds | 2 teaspoons honey *or* sugar |
| 1 teaspoon peppercorns | 4 tablespoons wine vinegar |

Pound the mustard seeds and peppercorns. Put them in a small bowl with the rest of the ingredients and mix together thoroughly. Put in small jars, seal and store in a cool, dry place.

This sweet-sour mustard is of course not designed to replace the pungent mustard mixture made simply of mustard powder and water.

# HERB MUSTARD

These mixtures are useful in adding to dressings or as a table mustard with hot or cold meats. Make with one or more dry herbs or very finely chopped fresh herbs. Add the mustard powder to the salt, herb or wine vinegar, herbs, sugar, pepper and olive oil. Stir together and add enough cold water to make a stiff paste. Put in small jars, seal and store in a cool, dry place.

| | |
|---|---|
| 3 tablespoons mustard powder | ½ teaspoon herbs |
| ½ teaspoon salt | ½ teaspoon sugar |
| 1½ teaspoons herb vinegar *or* wine vinegar | pinch of freshly ground pepper |
| | 1½ teaspoons olive oil |

# SUNDERLAND SPICE

This excellent savoury spice mixture is said to have originated in the North in the eighteenth century. Use for flavouring meat, stews, fish dishes and potted meats.

| | |
|---|---|
| 2 teaspoons peppercorns | 1 teaspoon freshy grated |
| 1 teaspoon broken mace | nutmeg |
| 1 teaspoon cloves | ¼–½ teaspoon chilli powder |

Grind together the peppercorns, mace, cloves, nutmeg and chilli powder. Bottle immediately after mixing in small dry pots. Store in a cool, dark place.

# Bibliography

Acton, Eliza, *Modern Cookery* (London, 1845)

Apicius, *The Roman Cookery of Apicius* (English translation by John Edwards (Rider, 1985)

Baker, Margaret, *Folklore and Customs of Rural England* (David & Charles, 1974)

Battam, Anne, *The Lady's Assistant in the Oeconomy of the Table* (London, 1759)

Beeton, Isabella, *The Book of Household Management* (London, 1861)

Bishop Frederick, *The Illustrated London Cookery Book* (London, 1852)

Blencowe, A., *The Receipt Book* (1694)

Boorde, Andrew, *A Dyetary of Helth* (1542)

Boxer, Arabella and Phillippa Black, *The Herb Book* (Octopus Books, 1980)

Briggs, Richard, *The English Art of Cookery* (London, 1788)

Buttes, Henry, *Dyets Dry Dinner* (1599)

Buttes, Henry, *Compleat Cook* (1655)

Clare, John, *The Shepherd's Calendar* (Oxford, 1964)

Cole, Mary, *Mrs Cole's Cookery* (3rd edition, London, 1791)

Copley, Esther, *The Complete Cottage Cookery* (11th edition, London, 1859)

Evelyn, John, *Acetaria* (1699)

Farley, John, *The London Art of Cookery* (London, 1783)

Gerard, John, *The Herball* (1597)

Glasse, Hannah, *The Art of Cookery Made Plain and Easy* (London, 1747)

Hall, T., *The Queen's Royal Cookery* (London, 1719)

Hartley, Dorothy, *Food in England* (Macdonald, 1954)

Heal, Carolyn and Michael Allsop, *Cooking with Spices* (David & Charles, 1983)

Heaton, Nell, *Traditional Recipes of the British Isles* (Faber & Faber, 1951)

Jennings, James, *Two Thousand Five Hundred Practical Recipes in Family Cookery* (London, 1844)

Markham, Gervase, *The English Hus-wife* (1615)

May, Robert, *The Accomplisht Cook* (1665)

Misson de Valbourg, Henri, *Memoirs and Observations in His Travels over England*, translated by J. Ozell (1719)

Raffald, Elizabeth, *The Experienced English Housekeeper* (1769)

Rundell, Mrs, *A New System of Domestic Cookery* (1835)

Smith, Eliza, *The Compleat Housewife* (1750)

Stobart, Tom, *Herbs, Spices and Flavourings* (David & Charles, 1970)

Tannahill, Reay, *Food in History* (Eyre Methuen, 1973)

Wilson, C. Anne, *Food and Drink in Britain* (Constable, 1973)

# Index